THE BUILDINGS OF
AN INDUSTRIAL COMMUNITY

Coalbrookdale and Ironbridge

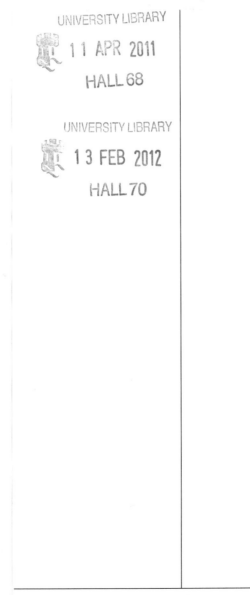

The Buildings of
an Industrial Community

COALBROOKDALE
and
IRONBRIDGE

W. Grant Muter

Published in association with
Ironbridge Gorge Museum Trust
by

Phillimore

1979

Published by
PHILLIMORE & CO. LTD.
London and Chichester
Head Office: Shopwyke Hall,
Chichester, Sussex, England

ISBN 0 85033 342 3

Printed in Great Britain by
UNWIN BROTHERS LIMITED
at The Gresham Press, Old Woking, Surrey
and bound by
THE NEWDIGATE PRESS LTD.
at Book House, Dorking, Surrey

To
R.A.H.

There are many things to be seen today which are not likely to be seen in ten years time, except in museums. There is smoke, a common thing today, but we do not know how soon it may be done away with. One touch of the magic wand of science and the chimneys and chimney pots will be useless clay . . . if our cameras do not catch these passing shadows, they will soon be forgotten.—*Frank Meadow Sutcliffe.*[1]

CONTENTS

LIST OF PLATES
(between pages 16 and 17)

I would like to thank the Shropshire Local History Library for permission to reproduce Plates 18, 19 and 45; the National Monuments Record for Plate 37, and the Ironbridge Gorge Museum Trust for Plates 1, 2, 20, 100 and 101.

LIST OF FIGURES

FOREWORD

It was in November 1973 that I began this study, which was to take two years to complete. The Fritz Thyssen Foundation of West Germany gave a grant towards the cost, and the fieldwork was undertaken from the headquarters of the Ironbridge Gorge Museum Trust. The publication was made possible by a grant from the Radcliffe Trust.

From the outset the idea was to widen the normal approach and concentrate not only on the large architect-designed houses, but to extend the survey to cover the large mass of buildings erected before 1914. That included small houses and cottages, farm buildings, public houses, hotels, shops, terraced rows, chapels, schools, and workhouses. Wherever possible I wanted also to link wider social and economic issues to the architectural theme, so that the buildings could be seen in a wider setting.

The Severn Gorge is something of a freak survival. The decline which set in after 1880 effectively froze the valley in its late-Victorian state. Very little new building took place, and up until the late 1960s, there were few of the usual pressures for renewal and redevelopment. That changed dramatically with the designation of the new town of Dawley, later Telford, in 1963, and the Gorge now stands on the perimeter of a vast new city which dwarfs the surrounding country. Descending into Coalbrookdale from Telford is now rather like entering Samuel Butler's *Erewhon.*

Many houses are empty or semi-derelict, whilst others are being renovated and modernised. Much of interest still stands, but some very poor modern development and indifferent restoration have spoilt parts. I was quite often sidetracked into looking at buildings that were being demolished, or recording interiors that were vanishing. The present economic situation has slowed the rate of restoration work, and much may now be saved that otherwise would have been lost.

I was refused entry into one house only, and everyone was almost without exception friendly and helpful. Many people assisted me during the work, including Mr. N. Cossons, Mr. B. Trinder, Mr. S. B. Smith, Dr. R. W. Brunskill, Dr. J. E. C. Peters, and Mr. H. King. I also wish to thank the staff of the Shropshire and County Record Office. The Local History Section of Shrewsbury Borough Library, and the library of The Institute of Advanced Architectural Studies at York. Lastly, I am indebted to Mr. S. Walker who developed and printed the photographs with meticulous care.

xv

The photographs convey the aesthetic quality of what can be seen much better than the text. I used a Pentax SP II camera, with a range of 28mm. f3.5, 55mm. f1.8, and 200mm. f4 lenses, and Kodak Tri-X and Ilford FP4 film. If I have not always had the opportunity of asking owners for permission to reproduce photographs of their houses I hope they will forgive me, and take the inclusion as a compliment. The line drawings are intended to illustrate particular points made in the text. I hope that one day it may be possible to add an accurate plan showing the original design of Coalport, but a good deal of documentary research first needs to be done.

Perhaps I should conclude this section by pointing out that this book is essentially concerned with buildings. No attempt has been made to record or discuss the outstanding industrial or civil engineering structures, such as the Iron Bridge or the Bedlam Furnaces, which are the most famous landmarks in the valley. These monuments have been documented and recorded at length already and I can see little point in duplicating the literature which is available elsewhere, and which, in any case, would have been beyond the strict limits of my original task. I suppose that in the last resort buildings hold a peculiar fascination for me, and I cannot help agreeing with Leonard Woolf when he says that 'what cuts deepest channels in our lives are the different houses in which we live—deeper even than "marriage and death and division" '.[2]

1. M. Hiley, *Frank Sutcliffe* (1974), pp. 137-8.
2. L. Woolf, *Beginning Again* (1964), p. 62.

INTRODUCTION

The Severn Gorge forms one of the most striking and distinctive landscapes in England (Fig. 1). From the wide open plain above Buildwas, the River Severn cuts its way into a narrow channel between the steep slopes of the Gorge, threading its way along banks covered with handging woodland and small cottages, for a distance of some three miles, until it opens out again in the flat rolling countryside downstream towards Bridgnorth.

It is a remarkable setting, made famous in the first decades of the 18th century by its early industrial development. The significance of Coalbrookdale, a small tributary valley leading off the Gorge, as a pioneering centre of industrialisation in Great Britain is now firmly established. It was an ideal site for the growth of the iron industry, possessing in close proximity good supplies of iron ore, coal, charcoal and water power, and within easy reach of the navigable waterway of the Severn. It was these advantages that the Quaker ironmaster, Abraham Darby, successfully exploited after evolving in 1709 a new technique for smelting iron ore, using coke instead of the traditional charcoal. The impact of this technological innovation was not immediate, and the rapid growth of industry in Coalbrookdale did not take place until over half a century later. By then the ironworks had become one of the largest in England, attracting travellers from all over the world.

During the early years of the 19th century the Coalbrookdale ironworks fell into relative decline. Other centres, such as South Wales and the Black Country, led the way. It was not until the middle of the century that Coalbrookdale experienced a period of economic expansion when its activity was concentrated largely on the manufacture of decorative and architectural castings. But by this time the centre of industry had shifted to the northern parts of the Shropshire coalfield, away from the Severn.

The 1850s saw the emergence of the clay industry in the Severn Gorge. This was largely concentrated on the south bank of the Severn in the towns of Jackfield and Broseley, upstream from the already well-established china works at Coalport. Here deposits of good quality clay were found in workable quantities. Bricks were produced in both towns, but the latter were renowned especially for their excellent roofing tiles, and two firms, Craven Dunnill, and Maw, specialised in decorative tile manufacture.

Today many monuments of this early industrial growth can still be seen. The most famous remains are the Abraham Darby furnace at Coalbrookdale, the first Iron Bridge, built in 1779, and the Bedlam furnaces. But there also

1

survives much of the industrial environment, rows of terraced workers' houses, and the larger houses of the ironmasters and managers, churches, chapels, schools, and public houses. These buildings were not obliterated by large-scale urban development in the 19th century. It is these smaller, but no less interesting structures, that are the subject of this study. Over one thousand buildings of pre–1914 date survive and these are concentrated in four main settlements: the town of Ironbridge, which is the centre of population; the valley of Coalbrookdale, to the north-west; and the villages of Jackfield and Coalport to the east.

Chapter One

PATTERN OF SETTLEMENT

The small town of Coalport was a deliberate piece of urban planning, one of the few specially created inland canal ports of the Industrial Revolution.[1] Originally it acted as a terminus of the Shropshire Canal, and formed a canal-river interchange for the transport of coal and other bulk materials. The town was the creation of the Shropshire ironmaster, William Reynolds, who leased the land in 1793. He quickly set about an ambitious building programme erecting a warehouse, wharves, quays, landing-places, and also cottages for workers. In 1802, Thomas Telford states that 30 houses had been built,[2] and shortly afterwards in 1803-4 a new terrace was completed, known locally as Smelthouse Row.[3] A new porcelain works was built in the west end of the village in 1796, and there were also rope, chain, and timber works.

By contrast, the Coalbrookdale valley (Plate 1) was never developed to a definite plan. Consequently the valley still retains some of the qualities of a rural village, and industrial development has never obliterated the gardens, orchards, and fields along its length. The Coalbrookdale ironworks never had total ownership and control of the land, and consequently, it was not able to design the layout rigidly to any preconceived plan. Building took place as the need arose on the sites that were then available. Development tended to be unco-ordinated, with building taking place on small, isolated plots which were scattered informally along the valley. The result was the gradual evolution of a low-density, linear settlement having no recognisable centre. Instead buildings flanked the furnaces, forges, pools and workings, along the total length of the valley.

The town of Ironbridge (Plate 2) had a very clearly identifiable centre, focused on a small group of buildings to the north of the Iron Bridge (Fig. 2). The *Tontine* hotel was carefully sited on a strategic frontage facing the northern approach road to the bridge, and to the east of the hotel a Market Square was laid out. Along the northern side of the Square, a large Market Building was erected, and on its eastern side a smaller Butter Market. This layout possibly formed part of a two-stage plan executed between *c.*1784-90 by the trustees of the Iron Bridge, who seem to have had a wide influence on local affairs.[4] There had been earlier developments in Ironbridge, notably in the area of Madeley Wood, and there was a great boom in building activity in the first decades of the 19th century, but these were haphazard and informal, with houses and shops built alongside existing roadways and along the contours of the hillside. They were not planned in the same way as the town centre.

The construction of the Severn Valley Railway through Ironbridge in 1862 was too late to shift development across the river on to the south bank. There was very little new building in the vicinity of the railway station. In contrast the impact of the railway on the town of Jackfield was dramatic, and the new line sliced straight through the heart of the existing settlement, splitting it in two.

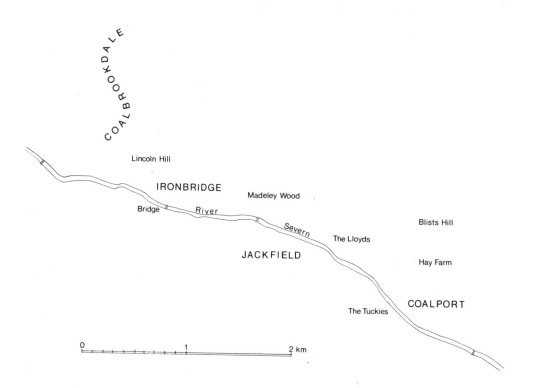

Fig. 1   The Severn Gorge: towns and settlements

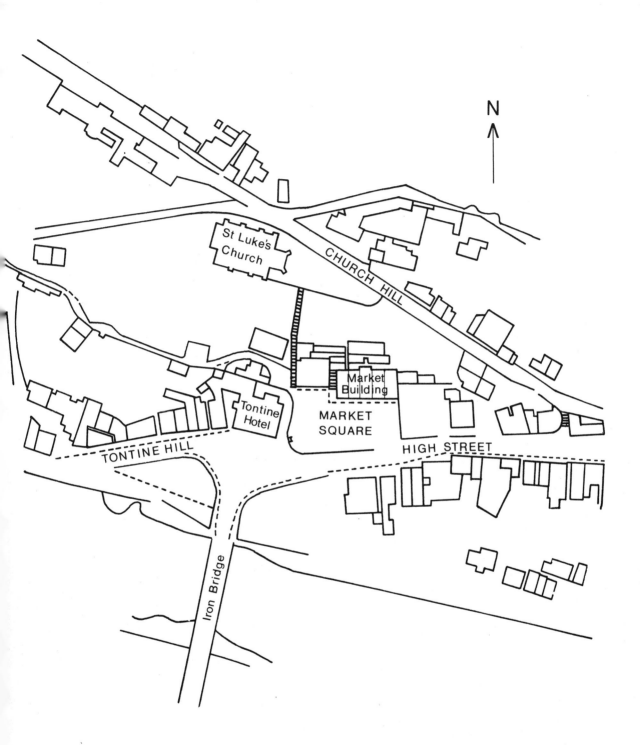

Fig. 2   Ironbridge Town Centre

5

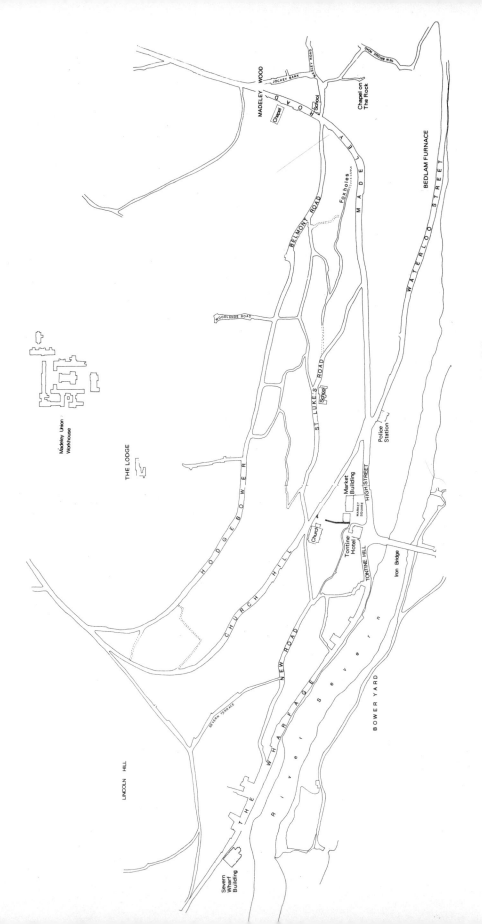

Fig. 3 The town of Ironbridge: major routes and buildings.

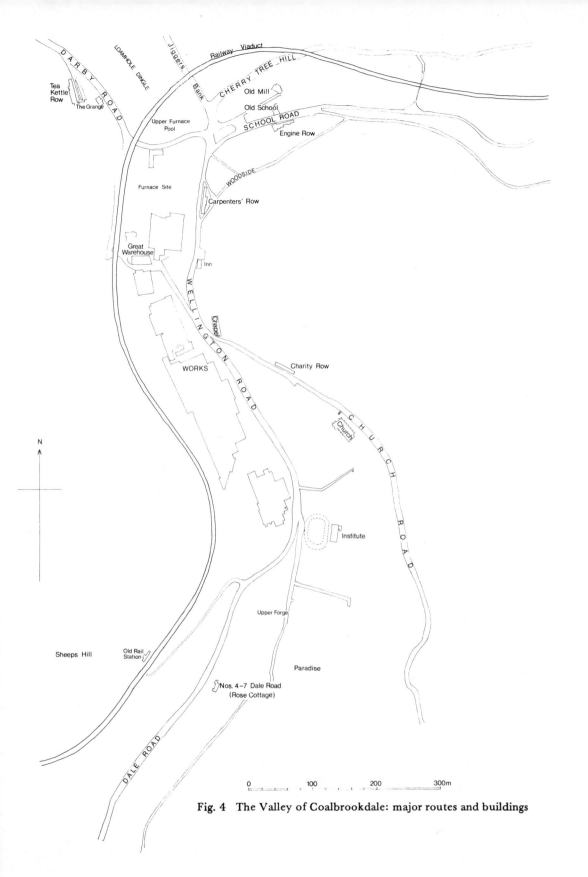

Fig. 4   The Valley of Coalbrookdale: major routes and buildings

Chapter Two

GROWTH AND DEVELOPMENT

'Here we may say is the merchantile part of the town of Madeley', wrote the Shrewsbury topographer, Charles Hulbert, of Ironbridge, in 1837, 'and here is the focus of professional and commercial pursuits. The weekly market, the Post Office, the Printing Office, principal inns, Drapery, Grocery and Ironmongery, Watch Making, Cabinet Making, Timber and Boat Building establishments; Subscription Library, Subscription Dispensary, Branch Bank, Subscription Baths, Gentlemen of the Legal and medical professions, Ladies Boarding School, etc. Navigation being also . . . carried on . . . gives to Ironbridge the character and appearance of an inland port.'[5]

The town of Ironbridge in 1840 with a population of a little over 4,000 was at its zenith. Its importance as a market town and communications centre had been secured in 1779 by the completion of the Iron Bridge and its strategic position close to the navigable River Severn had encouraged a rapid expansion between 1810 and 1840, linked closely with the rising fortunes of the local clay industry. A church had been built on an improbable site high up on the steep slopes of the Gorge. The tower had been placed at the east end as the surrounding ground was unstable. The heart of the town, around the Market Square, was already well established, and there was a continuous stretch of development along the riverside as far as Coalbrookdale.[6]

The most fashionable residential area rose behind the Market Square along the steep roadway of Church Hill and along the hilltop at Hodgebower (Fig. 3). Here the large houses of the professional and servant-keeping classes were built in a variety of styles. Fanciful Gothic villas were erected—the kind of houses that were also being built in the suburbs of many provincial English cities. Some residences were loosely in the style of the Greek Revival, others were more conventional, imitating the domestic grandeur of the 18th century.

The great period of expansion in Coalbrookdale had long since passed. It corresponded with the dramatic growth of the ironworks in the decades following 1770. Some idea of the extent of this development is given by contemporary maps. A plan of Coalbrookdale dated 1753 shows a cluster of buildings below the Upper Forge Pool[7]—Darby's old house, a stable, several tenements, and a forge—and another group of buildings below the Upper Furnace Pool, but the development is small in scale and relatively thin. Coalbrookdale in the mid-18th century was still a small, comparatively undeveloped valley.

Compare this with the extensive settlement that had grown up by 1794. By then all the terraced rows had been built, there was more development below the Upper Furnace Pool, Darby Road was established as the fashionable residential area, and there was a continuous thread of small cottages and houses along the whole length of the valley. This boom in building activity seems to have coincided with the rapid expansion of the ironworks in the final quarter of the 18th century, and lasted until the trade recession of 1794.

During the early 19th century a number of small houses were built on the higher slopes of the valley, and in the small area of Paradise (Fig. 4). The larger houses, mostly built towards the middle of the century, tended to be concentrated in Church Road, at Dale End, and the head of the valley. The largest buildings, the church and the institute, were not built until the 1850s and were amongst the last buildings to be erected. Surprisingly, the construction of the Wenlock and Severn Junction Railway in 1864 did not generate a wave of new building activity. By this date development had already begun to peter out.

By 1793 the Shropshire Canal extended from the towns of Donnington Wood, through Oakengates and Stirchley, to the River Severn. Its completion stimulated the growth of Coalport, and resulted in a large increase in the sale of coal from the town, whose industries included the famous china works. In the mid-19th century there were 500 inhabitants, the works employed 500 hands, many of whom lived in Broseley and Madeley, and a small Wesleyan chapel, an infant school, and a literary and artistic institute had been built.[8]

The development of the clay industries on the south bank of the Severn during the late 18th century, resulted in the renewed growth of the town of Jackfield.[9] Building in the 18th century had been concentrated along the riverside and on the adjacent plateau running above it. With the growth of the large encaustic tile works of Maw and Co., and Craven Dunnill, development shifted to the western end of the town, and new terraces were built in close proximity to the works.

Chapter Three

BUILDING TYPES

The most prominent individual buildings in the Severn Gorge are the large churches, chapels, schools, and commercial buildings, which form a distinctive feature in the townscape of each settlement. The Gorge is rich in these 19th-century buildings, and the varied architecture with which the area abounds is at least partly derived from the variations in their style and the use of different building materials in their construction.

A whole range of different styles was in fashion at successive periods throughout the 19th century. In the 1830s Gothic was still in favour, and the most distinguished ecclesiastical building of the time, St. Luke's church, Ironbridge, is designed in the Early English style. From the late 1850s onwards, there is a change to Tudor Gothic and the Elizabethan styles, as exemplified by two notable buildings, the Coalbrookdale Scientific and Literary Institute (1859), and Ironbridge National School (1859). Later the Italianate style is in use, and Ironbridge Police Station (1862) is an interesting example of a leading national style, as interpreted by a local firm of architects and builders. Generally the designs in Ironbridge and Coalbrookdale tend to be conservative by national standards, running some way behind the more advanced architectural thinking of a journal like *The Builder.*

Industrial patronage was a powerful force in Coalbrookdale in the 18th and 19th centuries. Because of its isolated semi-rural position, the valley lacked any of the important amenities to be found in an established town. It therefore fell on the ironworks to provide these, and the Company thus became involved in the provision of a range of buildings outside the workplace. This included not only company housing, but also a shop, a school, a church and a public house. The last important building erected by the Coalbrookdale Company was the Literary and Scientific Institute, built in 1859.

Industrial patronage never entirely died out. The Madeley Wood Company gave £1,000 towards the cost of St. Luke's church, Ironbridge, in 1837,[10] and later Jackfield church was built with the aid of endowments from local industry. But as the 19th century progressed the State began to replace the industrialist as patron. Partly this process was a result of national legislation. For the first time government funds were available for a variety of public buildings. New churches were built following the Church Building Act of 1818, new schools were constructed with grant aids following the education Act of 1833, and after the Poor Law Act of 1834, new workhouses began to be erected. The State became a major patron.[11]

At the same time the demand for qualified architects to design these new buildings was on the increase. At the beginning of the 19th century most of the commissions were awarded to local architects and surveyors, but after 1850 important work was given to men from London, the most notable being Arthur Blomfield, who designed St. Mary's, Jackfield, in 1862.

The most successful local firm of building contractors in the mid-19th century was Nevett Brothers of Ironbridge. This firm built the Wesleyan Infant School, Madeley Wood (1858), the church of St. Mary, Jackfield (1863), and the Madeley Union Workhouse (1874). In addition Samuel Nevett was architect as well as contractor for the Ironbridge National School (1859), and Ironbridge Police Station (1862).

Churches

In 1818 the first Church Building Act set aside one million pounds for building new churches, particularly in the rapidly-expanding industrial towns, where it was felt that there was not proper accommodation for the new industrial classes.[12] Later a second parliamentary grant of two million pounds was made, following the windfall repayment by Austria of a war-time loan that had been written off as lost. It was with the aid of a £200 grant from this source, and a further grant of £800 from the Incorporated Church Building Society, that the church of St. Luke, Ironbridge, was built.[13] Funds were controlled by Commissioners appointed under the Act, and the churches built as a result of the Act came to be known as 'Commissioners' Churches'. Money was limited, and, like other Commissioners' churches, St. Luke's had to be built as cheaply as possible. Consequently architectural elaboration was minimal.

The **Church of St. Luke, Ironbridge** (Plate 3), stands on the south side of Church Hill, on the steep hillside above the Iron Bridge. The foundation stone was laid on 13 July 1835, and the church was completed in 1837. The architect and contractor was Thomas Smith of Madeley,[14] and the total cost £3,232 1s. 11d.[15]

It is a good example of a Commissioners' church, and illustrates the economy with which these buildings were typically constructed. The exterior is very plain, and buttresses do not rise above the parapet. The tower has simple clasping buttresses, battlements and pinnacles. Ornament is largely confined to Gothic detailing and brick hood moulds. This gives the exterior a somewhat stark appearance.

The ground plan is rectangular, with a sanctuary recess at the west end, and a tower to the east. The normal order is reversed because of problems of instability. The nave (Plate 4) has three bays, each with paired lancets, and galleries supported by slender cast-iron columns manufactured by the Coalbrookdale Company. The three lancets in the east window (Plate 5) are by Evans of Shrewsbury, and depict St. John the Evangelist, St. James the Great, and St. Peter.

11

The **Church of Holy Trinity, Coalbrookdale** (Plate 6), lies on the south side of Church Road, Coalbrookdale. It is built of local Dawley stone with roofs of slate. The foundation stone was laid on 11 December 1851, and the church consecrated on 25 July 1854. The Architects were Reeves and Voysey of London, the contractor W. Hinley of Coalbrookdale, and Abraham Darby donated £6,000 towards the cost.[16]

The church is designed in the decorated style of the Gothic revival. The plan consists of chancel, nave with side aisles, and tower at the south-west angle. The windows to each bay have curvilinear tracery, and one in the south aisle incorporates a 16th-century panel of Flemish glass depicting the last supper (Plate 7). The nave (Plate 8) has an open-timbered roof, an octagonal font in south aisle, and bench ends manufactured by the London Patent Carving Company. The chancel was restored by Goodhart Rendel in 1932. In the burial ground are a few cast-iron tomb-plates (Plate 9).

The **Church of St. Mary, Jackfield** (Plate 10 and Fig. 5) stands in a small churchyard on the southern banks of the Severn. It has walls of polychrome brickwork, with Grinshill stone dressings, and roofs of geometrical tiling. The foundation stone was laid on 16 October 1862, and the building consecrated on 20 August 1863. The architect was A. W. Blomfield, and the cost estimated at £2,500.[17]

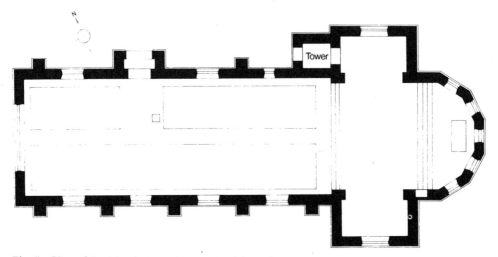

Fig. 5 Plan of St. Mary's Church, Jackfield (1863)

The style is French Gothic and idiosyncratic. A similar church had been designed by Street at Howsham, Yorkshire, in 1859.[18] The plan is cruciform and consists of a nave chancel with apse, and transepts (Fig. 5). A small engaged tower rises to form an octagonal lantern, with surrounding columns, and a steep conical roof. The inside walls are entirely faced with bare brick in bands of red and white; only the window jambs are plastered. The west window is circular, divided into 10 compartments by earthenware columns. The nave windows have geometrical tracery, and there are five lancets in the apse. The glass in the east windows is in the style of Heaton, Butler, and Bayne, and executed in vivid colours. The windows depict the Agony in the Garden, and Road to Golgotha, the Crucifixion, the Deposition, and the Resurrection.

Chapels and Meeting Houses

Nonconformist buildings were designed with neat classical fronts and plain sides. The severity of the exteriors was matched by the sparse decoration of the interiors. The earlier chapels have a vernacular simplicity and delicate detailing which is lacking in the heavy monumentality of the later 19th century.

Competition from the Church of England increased during the new wave of Anglican church building in the Victorian period. The Wesleyan Methodist chapel at Madeley Wood, and the church of St. Luke, Ironbridge, were completed within a few months of each other in 1837. There were surprising similarities in design. Interiors were box-like, with galleries built along the walls to accommodate as many worshippers as possible, and financial stringency reduced ornament to a bare minimum.

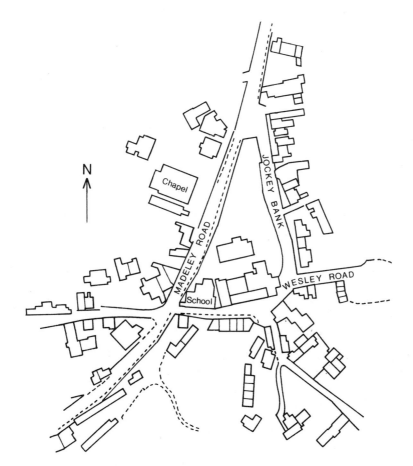

Fig. 6 Madeley Wood

Madeley Wood was the traditional centre of Nonconformism in the Gorge. A small stone cottage which became known as **The Chapel on the Rock** (Plate 11) was built *c.* 1700 on a spur overlooking the Severn.[19] This may be the three-storey house which survives next to Nos. 52–53 New Bridge Road. It continued in use until John Fletcher, Methodist vicar of Madeley from 1760 to 1785, initiated the building of a new [Wesleyan] chapel in 1776. This small single-storey building of brick, three bays long, with round arched window openings and stone lintels with keyblocks, still stands in the grounds of the former Wesleyan Infant school. The original entrance in the west gable is blocked, but above the arched door opening is a rectangular tablet and small semi-circular window. Nearby, at the Foxholes, a small chapel erected by the **Wesleyan New Connection** formerly stood,[20] but this has now been demolished.

Across the river in Jackfield lies the **Wesleyan Chapel, Coalford**, a small single-storey building in brick, erected in 1825. The entrance doorway in the north gable is flanked by tall narrow window openings with elliptical heads. The windows are cast-iron and the side elevation is of three bays, each having windows recessed between plain brick pilasters.

The largest Nonconformist building erected prior to 1850 is the **Wesleyan Methodist Chapel, Madeley Wood** (Plate 12 and Fig. 6), dated 1837. It was designed by Samuel Smith of Madeley and cost an estimated £1,590.[21] The street front has a pedimental gable, with plain entablature, and stone coping. The central entrance forms part of a symmetrical elevation and is emphasised by a heavy stone door-case with deep cornice. Windows are cast-iron and recessed beneath over-arches of brick. On the ground floor the openings are rectangular; on the second storey semi-circular. The interior has side galleries, supported by slender cast-iron pillars. These are approached by a staircase from the entrance lobby.

The last chapel to be built in the Severn Gorge was the **Fletcher Memorial Wesleyan Chapel, Coalbrookdale** (Plate 13), dated 1885. It stands on a prominent site at the west end of Church Road, and faces south. A small brick chapel, built in 1785, was demolished to make way for it.[22] The front has none of the robust simplicity of this earlier chapel and the design typifies the highly-ornamented Italianate style of the late 19th century. The main features of the gabled front are semi-circular windows with keyblocks and a large two-storey entrance porch with semi-circular arched doorway. The interior has been converted for use as a warehouse and all the fittings removed. The upper chapel was originally approached by a pair of staircases that flanked the entrance lobby.

The **Friends' Meeting House** in Coalbrookdale formerly stood in Darby Road, and was built in 1789.[23] It has been demolished, but a small burial-ground to the rear of the site survives.

Public Buildings

A town hall was never built in either Coalbrookdale or Ironbridge. There is nothing to compare with the monumental public buildings erected in the industrial north in the mid-19th century. There are, however, two public buildings of note—a workhouse, and a police station—both in the town of Ironbridge.

The former **Madeley Union Workhouse** (Plate 14), now the Beeches Hospital, stands on a site of nearly eight acres on the summit of Lincoln Hill to the north of the town of Ironbridge. It replaced an older workhouse that formerly stood at the east end of Hodgebower. Part of this range of buildings survives as Nos. 4–11 Belmont Road.

The new workhouse was built in 1874. The architects were Messrs. Haddon of Great Malvern, the contractor Samuel Nevett of Ironbridge,[24] and the cost of the building was £13,800.[25] It is a plain design, in polychrome brick, with little architectural elaboration. Decoration is largely confined to the enrichment of window heads, polychrome string courses and stone dressings. Buildings are grouped in blocks around a central quadrangle, which is approached from the west beneath a segmented archway. The original layout comprised a board-room, clerks' office on the right of the entrance, and guest-rooms on the left. The dining-rooms, a laundry, wash-house, workshops and dormitories formed a separate complex around the inner yard, with the infirmary along the east side.[26]

The former **Police Station** (Plate 15) at Ironbridge, lies on the south side of Waterloo Street, at the junction of the Madeley and Coalport Roads. The building is of blue brick with white brick quoins and dressings of Grinshill stone. The building was opened in November 1862, and Samuel Nevett of Ironbridge was both architect and contractor.[27]

The police station is one of the few Italianate designs in the Gorge. The lower storey is an open arcade, composed of a series of four segmental arches, each with a central keyblock, supported by brick piers with stone dressings. The upper storey has moulded stone architraves which match the lower arches. The internal layout originally consisted of a magistrates' room, three cells, a police residence and additional underground vaults.

The former **Dispensary and Savings Bank**, built in 1828,[28] has been demolished. It stood in an important position opposite the police station on a triangular plot of land at the base of Church Hill.

Commercial and Industrial Buildings

During the late 18th and early 19th centuries Ironbridge was renowned as a thriving market town, with shops in all branches of the retail trade. It was a focus of commercial activity and many good buildings of this period survive. The most distinguished is the **Market Building** (Nos. 2–6 Market Square), Ironbridge (Plate 16 and Fig. 7). The central bay breaks forward slightly, and the pediment incorporates an oval window. The first, third and fifth bays each have tripartite Palladian windows to the first floor. These are over-arched on the second floor, where the sills form a continuous string band across the width of the front. The ground floor has five segmental arcaded arches, which were originally open, but are now filled with later shop fronts. The architect is not known, but may have been Samuel Wright of Kidderminster. The building probably dates from c. 1790.

The Market Building, Ironbridge

| 5 | 0 | 5 | 10 | 15 | Metres |

| 10 | 0 | 10 | 20 | 30 | 40 | 50 | Feet |

Fig. 7

G Muter 1974

A group of late 18th-century shops formerly stood opposite the *Tontine* hotel on the corner of the north-west abutment of the bridge. They had stucco fronts and balconettes on the first floor. They have now been demolished, but several good shop fronts have survived. Some in the High Street, Ironbridge, have cast-iron window lintels and sills. A late 18th-century front at No. 1 The Wharfage has its original bow-window and, nearer the Market Square, a collection of shops along Tontine Hill form a good townscape group. A polychrome Victorian front, *c.* 1860, at the bottom of Church Hill (No. 15 High Street) (Plate 17) has semi-circular toothed stone architraves to the first-floor windows.

Much of the commercial expansion of Ironbridge in the 19th century was concentrated along the wharves which lined the narrow riverside of the Severn. Warehouses and malthouses grew up along its length, and it became a centre of trading activity in the town. Visual evidence of this past commercial activity can be seen in surviving late 19th-century photographs (Plates 18 and 19), which show a number of warehouses fronting the river.[29] Those that survive are built as close to the road as possible, with the gable end facing the river. They are three storeys in height, and some have projecting sack hoists from the gable loft.

Two of the best warehouse designs were completed for the Coalbrookdale Company. The **Severn Wharf Building** (Plate 20) lies at the west end of The Wharfage, Ironbridge, and is a polychrome building in the Gothic style, built

16

1. General view of Coalbrookdale, looking north, *c.* 1890.

2. The Wharfage, Ironbridge, looking towards the Severn Warehouse, *c.* 1900.

3. Church of St. Luke, Ironbridge (1836).

4. Interior of Church of St. Luke, Ironbridge (1836).

5. Stained glass in Church of St. Luke, Ironbridge (1836).

6. Church of Holy Trinity, Coalbrookdale (1854).

7. Stained glass in Church of Holy Trinity, Coalbrookdale (1854).

8. Interior of Church of Holy Trinity, Coalbrookdale (1854).

9. (*above*) Tomb-plates in churchyard of Holy Trinity, Coalbrookdale (1854).

10. Church of St. Mary, Jackfield (1863).

CHAPELS

11. (*above left*) Chapel on the Rock, Madeley Wood (17th-century).

12. (*above*) Wesleyan Methodist Chapel, Madeley Wood (1837).

13. (*left*) Fletcher Memorial Wesleyan Chapel, Coalbrookdale (1885).

14.   Madeley Union Workhouse, Ironbridge (1874).

15.   Police station, Ironbridge (1862).

16. Market Building, Ironbridge (*c.*1790).

17. Victorian shop front, No. 15 High Street, Ironbridge.

18 & 19. Late 19th-century views of Ironbridge.

20. (*below*) Late 19th-century view of the Severn Wharf Building, Ironbridge.

21. (*top left*) The Great Warehouse, Coalbrookdale.
22. (*above*) Former Mill, Coalbrookdale.
23. (*below*) Maw & Co. Encaustic Tile Works, Jackfield.

INNS, HOTELS AND TAVERNS

24. (*above*) *Tontine* Hotel, Ironbridge (1783 and 1786).

25. (*below*) The *Boat* Inn, Jackfield.

EDUCATIONAL BUILDINGS

26. (*above*) Old School, Coalbrookdale.

27. (*right*) Wesleyan Infant School,
Madeley Wood (1858).

28. National School, Ironbridge (1859), ('The Blue School').

29. Coalbrookdale Literary & Scientific Institution (1859).

FARM BUILDINGS

30. (*top left*) Hay Farm, stable block (1775): ventilation openings to loft.

31. (*above*) Hay Farm, stable block (1775): ground floor louvred window.

32. (*left*) Hay Farm, stable block (1775): interior view of stalls.

33. (*below left*) The Lees, Coalport Road; range of farm buildings.

34. The Lodge, Ironbridge.

HOUSE ELEVATIONS

35. The Tuckies, Jackfield.

36. (*above*) Nos. 4–7 Dale Road, Coalbrookdale
(Rose Cottage).

37. The Grange, Darby Road, Coalbrookdale,
(Rosehill House).

38.   The Calcutts House, Jackfield (1775).

39.   Belmont House, Ironbridge (1753).

40. (*left*) No. 54 New Bridge Road, Ironbridge.

41. (*right*) No. 1 St. Luke's Road, Ironbridge.

42. (*left*) Primrose Cottage, Jiggers Bank, Coalbrookdale.

43. No. 24 Belmont Road, Ironbridge.

44. Nos. 14–15 Woodlands Road, Ironbridge.

45.   Cottages grouped in pairs at Dale End (photograph *c.*1900).

46.   Range of cottages, Jackfield (1750).

47. Nos. 44–46 Wellington Road, Coalbrookdale.

48. Nos. 52–54 Wellington Road, Coalbrookdale.

49. (*left*) Nos. 2–6 New Road, Ironbridge.

50. (*right*) No. 8 New Road, Ironbridge.

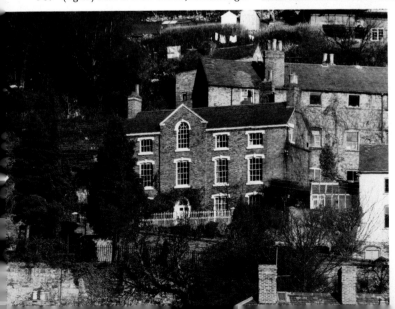

51. (*left*) South View, Church Hill, Ironbridge

USE OF ROOMS IN HOUSES

52. (*above*) Living room of cottage, Coalbrookdale.

53. (*left*) Panelling in parlour of cottage at Ironbridge.

54. Setlas in kitchen of cottage in Bridge Road, Benthall, Broseley.

55. Pair of mid 17th-century stone cottages, 58–59 Hodgebower, Ironbridge.

56. Nailor's Row, Ironbridge (late 19th-century view).

TERRACED HOUSING IN THE COALBROOKDALE VALLEY

57. (*left*) Tea Kettle Row, Coalbrookdale.

58. (*below*) Carpenters' Row, Coalbrookdale.

59. (*left*) Engine Row, Coalbrookdale.

MATERIALS AND CONSTRUCTION

60. (*above*) Wattle and daub panel at Nos. 4–7 Dale Road, Coalbrookdale.

61. (*left*) Stone base to brick wall at the Tuckies House, Jackfield.

62. (*below*) Polychrome roof at Nos. 20–21 Buildwas Road, Ironbridge.

ARCHITECTURAL DETAILS

(i) DATED FEATURES

63. (*above*) Cartouche at Belmont House, Belmont Road, Ironbridge.

64. Dated lead rainwater head, Calcutts House, Jackfield.

65. (*right*) Double-light mullion and transom window.

66. Tripartite Palladian window, the Market Building, Ironbridge.

67. Sash window with skewback lintel and fluted keyblock.

68. Sash window with simulated voussoirs to lintel.

69. Sash window with moulded segmental-arched lintel and keyblock.

70. Sash window with rectangular lintel with sunk panels.

71. Cast-iron window, No. 1 Cherry Tree Hill, Coalbrookdale.

72. Cast-iron window, former mill, Coalbrookdale.

73. Cast-iron lintel and sill,
No. 31 Wellington Road, Coalbrookdale.

74. Cast-iron window with fanlight head, Ironbridge.

75. (*above*) 19th-century Gothic-style window with brick label moulds.

76. Greek Revival-style window, No. 57 Belmont Road, Ironbridge.

77. Door-case at Paradise House, Coalbrookdale.

78. Plain door-case with simple entablature, No. 5 New Road, Ironbridge.

79. Door-case with moulded pilasters, No. 11 Paradise, Coalbrookdale.

80. Door-case at The Lees, Coalport Road, Madeley.

81. (*above left*) Door canopy, No. 53 Wellington Road, Coalbrookdale.

82. (*above*) Cast-iron porch, Woodside House, Coalbrookdale.

83. (*left*) Entrance doorway, *Tontine* Hotel, Ironbridge.

84.   Dentil eaves.

85.   Bricks set diagonally at eaves.

86.   Moulded brick course at eaves.

87. Chimney-stacks at Hay House, Madeley.

88. Group of chimney-stacks along The Wharfage, Ironbridge.

89. (*above*) Castellated turrets, Severn Wharf Building, Ironbridge.

90. (*above right*) Spirally-grooved shafts with chevron patterning, Orchard House, Ironbridge.

91. (*right*) Cast-iron chimney 'pots', Coalbrookdale.

92.   Interior view showing valley boards supporting gable roof.

(vi) ROOF STRUCTURES

(vii) STAIRCASES

93. (*above*) The Tuckies House, Jackfield (17th century).

94. (*left*) The Calcutts House, Jackfield (1755).

95. *Tontine* Hotel, Ironbridge (1783).

96. Coalbrookdale Company Offices,
Coalbrookdale.

(viii) FIREPLACES

97. (*above*) *Tontine* Hotel, Ironbridge (1786).

98. Fireplace with applied composition decoration to pinewood architrave, Ironbridge.

99. Carved mantel to cottage fireplace, Ironbridge.

100. *a.* and *b.* Cast-iron grates, 30 Wellington Road, Coalbrookdale.

101.   Cottage fireplace with cast-iron architrave.

102.   Cottage range.

103. Range with pot hook and brass stirrup drop handles.

104. Range with decoration on cove and oven front.

105. Oven door of range showing anthemion decoration.

106. Range with oven doors decorated with lions in relief.

107. Cellar at No. 11 Jockey Bank, Ironbridge.

(ix) OTHER ARCHITECTURAL DETAILS

108. Cottage locks.

109. (*above*) Door furniture: letterbox.

110. (*right*) Door furniture: door-knocker.

111. Door furniture: Norfolk latch.

112. Rainwater goods: wrought-iron gutter bracket.

113. (*left*) Cast-iron water conduit, Church Hill, Ironbridge.

114. (*above*) Cast-iron mile plate, The Wharfage, Ironbridge.

115. (*below*) Cast-iron boundary plate, High Street, Coalport.

GENERAL — STREET FURNITURE

116. (*left*) Wrought-iron gateway, Tontine Hill, Ironbridge.

117. (*below*) Wrought-iron gates, South View, Church Hill, Ironbridge.

prior to 1849.[30] It is constructed to a rectangular ground-plan with a small polygonal apse at its east end. The outer walls are castellated with pinnacles and buttresses, and the window openings are formed of pointed arches with hood moulds. The windows have solid cast-iron frames with lattice glazing. Two ornamental castellated turrets flank the apse at the east end.

The **Great Warehouse** (Plate 21), standing in the centre of the Coalbrookdale Company works, is a particularly good piece of industrial architecture in the functional tradition. The principal elevation is of nine bays, and each of the three floors has a series of cast-iron windows along its length. These have cast-iron lintels and also cast-iron sills. Each window is divided by a delicate grid of cast-iron glazing bars. Above the twin-span roof is a central cast-iron clock tower, dated 1843, which is supported by an ornamental base with splayed timber legs. Each face of the clock has enriched spandrels, and above is a shallow-hipped roof surmounted by a ball finial. The interior is not fireproof, having wooden floors supported by hollow cast-iron columns.[31]

The former corn-mill in Coalbrookdale (Nos. 1–3 **Mill House Cottages**, School Road) (Plate 22) has very similar window openings to the Great Warehouse, with cast-iron lintels and sills, and solid frame cast-iron windows (Fig. 28). The two buildings may be contemporary. The mill has been substantially altered in conversion to three dwellings, and a pediment removed from the main front.[32]

At Coalport two of the original bottle-shaped brick-kilns survive at the site of the former Coalport china works, now a museum. The adjacent buildings form part of the industrial complex. The other major group of industrial buildings is associated with the clay and tile industry across the river in Jackfield. Only a part of the works occupied by Maw and Company now stands, but this includes another characteristic warehouse in the functional tradition, complete with roofed sack-hoist (Plate 23). The factory of Craven Dunnill to the east is principally distinguished by the decorative tiling in the tympana of the window openings.

Inns, Hotels and Taverns

Hotels and inns formed important staging posts on road routes linking provincial towns in the 18th century. They were also important in the economy of many towns, and the carrying trade was organised around them. Sometimes they provided assembly rooms and served as public meeting-places, where administrative matters could be settled. Entertainment was another function they fulfilled.[33]

The principal inn within the Severn Gorge was the **Tontine Hotel**, Ironbridge (Plate 24).[34] It was advertised in the Dublin, Chester, Bath and Bristol newspapers,[35] and was considered convenient, being near to both Bridgnorth and Shrewsbury. The inn had all the facilities of a good staging post, including a stable block and an assembly room. The latter was used by the trustees of the Iron Bridge as a meeting-place.

The hotel was built c. 1785, and designed by John Hiram Haycock.[36] The south front faces the Iron Bridge, and is of five bays, having a central porch with broken pediment, radial fanlight and marginal side lights. This front was extended eastwards by two bays, and the side elevation remodelled, after 1786. A break in the wall-face between the third and fourth bays marks the line of the addition. The alteration gave the east front greater prominence. On this side the central bay breaks forward slightly, and has a circular window in the tympanum of the pediment, also a good tripartite Venetian window below. The dressings are of high-quality gauged brickwork. This extension may have been a collaboration of Haycock and his surveyor, Samuel Wright, of Kidderminster.[37]

There is another impressive hotel frontage in Ironbridge, at the **Crown Inn**, Hodgebower. This is a smaller building, of three bays, built in the early 19th century. It has three storeys and a central doorcase with broken pediment and radial fanlight. There were numerous other inns throughout the Gorge. Often the interiors have been refurbished and the original fittings destroyed. Most of these inns are smaller buildings which are vernacular in quality, like the *Boat* inn at Jackfield (Plate. 25).

Cassey's Directory (1874) lists 17 inns and taverns in Ironbridge, including: four at the Lloyds—the *Bird in Hand,* the *Blockhouse,* the *Lake Head,* the *Robin Hood*; three at Madeley Wood—the *Golden Ball,* the *Half Moon,* the *Unicorn*; three in Bridge Street—the *Retreat,* the *Three Tuns,* and the *Tontine* hotel; four on The Wharfage—the *Rodney,* the *Swan,* the *Talbot,* the *White Hart*; two on Lincoln Hill—the *Horse,* the *Swan*; and one, the *Royal Oak,* on Church Hill. In addition 13 beerhouses are listed.[38]

The ownership of inns was sometimes in the hands of industrial proprietors. The **Brewery Inn** at Coalport, for example, was the property of the china works, and in Coalbrookdale the **Commercial Hotel** (The Grove), licensed in 1839, was owned by the Coalbrookdale Company.[39] Industry was thus closely involved in the establishment and management of some public houses.

Educational Buildings

In some of the new industrial settlements employers provided schooling for apprentices. Factory owners thus became directly involved in the provision of education for their employees.[40] The Coalbrookdale Company supported a day-school for boys, at what is now the Old School House, Coalbrookdale. The exact date of its foundation is not known, but the company may have been among the pioneers in the field of early industrial schooling. It was certainly a pioneer of adult education, building in 1859 a new Literary and Scientific Institution for its workpeople.

The 19th century saw the rapid expansion of church school building by all the main religious denominations. School building came to be seen in much the same way as church building, as a means of spreading distinctive religious views throughout the new industrial areas.[41] The competition between the different religious factions was fierce. The local historian John Randall remarks on the extreme bitterness of the controversy and the unfair advantage that some sects sought to take of the local education movement.[42]

Intervention by the State began modestly in the early 19th century, but after 1833 assumed significant proportions, so that during the period between 1839

18

and 1859 government grant expenditure totalled £4.4 million, of which over £1 million was granted for enlarging and repairing elementary schools.[43] Detailed guidance to architects, builders, and school promoters was given by an official government body, the Committee of Council on Education, which set out rules for the submission of plans and issued recommendations on space standards and the layout of schools and classrooms.[44] By allocating conditional grants in this way the government exerted a considerable influence on internal design, and this can be seen in the layout and internal plan of two local schools built in Ironbridge in the late 1850s: the Wesleyan Infant school, Madeley Wood (1858), and the Ironbridge National school (1859).[45]

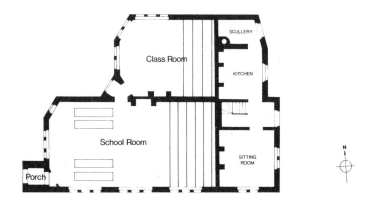

Fig. 8   (*above*) Plan of Madeley Wood School (1858);
(*below*) Ironbridge National School (1859)

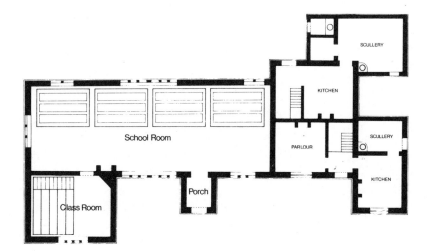

19

Elementary schools built in Ironbridge, Coalbrookdale and Jackfield in the second quarter of the nineteenth century are single-storey buildings built of brick. The style is somewhat Classical with pilasters and pediments, but Gothic features such as hood-moulds are also used. After 1850 Tudor Gothic first appears, and an extravagant polychrome design described as 'Early English'. In fact, strict historical accuracy is not followed in either style or detailing, the main aim being the creation of a general picturesque effect.

The **Old School, Coalbrookdale** (Plate 26), Nos. 1–2 School Road, lies beyond a small green at the head of the valley. The principal elevation, of three bays, faces south and the windows are of cast-iron with solid frames. Window heads are flat-arched on the ground floor, and round-arched above. Sills and lintels are also of cast-iron. The building is now divided into four separate dwellings.

A few small school buildings were erected during the second quarter of the 19th century and these were of the simplest kind, architectural embellishment being confined mostly to the use of moulded brick for detailing windows and doorways. The **Parochial Infant School, Ironbridge,** survives from this period. It is a single-storey building of brick and lies on the north side of Madeley Road. The school is dated 1831 and has transomed windows with brick hood-moulds. **Jackfield School** is of a similar style, with brick hood-moulds to the windows, and a prominent central entrance, complete with pediment, pilasters and a deep brick string-course. The front is dated 1844 and some of the external bricks are marked 'Taylor, Tuckies'. The **Coalbrookdale National School** dates from the mid-19th century, and is a two-storey building on the west side of Wellington Road, Coalbrookdale. Again the windows have deep brick hood-moulds, and the end gables have elaborate ornamental bargeboards. A small **Roman Catholic School** with a pyramidal roof stands on an isolated knoll on Sheep's Hill, near the end of the Dale.

The **Wesleyan Infant School, Madeley Wood** (Plate 27) was officially opened on 3 January 1859. It is the first of the large new schools built in the late 1850s and is richly decorated in polychrome brick. The roof is covered with ornamental bands of geometrical tiling. The architect was James Wilson of Bath, and the contractors Messrs. Nevett of Ironbridge. The building is reported to have cost £400.[46]

The front is styled in richly ornate Gothic, with a bell-turret at the west end. In the centre is a single-storey schoolroom, and the master's house is at the east end. The windows are generally two-and three-light lancets with polychrome brick arches. An oriel window on the second storey of the master's house has been replaced. Set into the west wall of the bell-tower is a stone tablet, dated 1858, commemorating the dedication of the school to the Rev. J. W. Fletcher of Madeley.

The internal layout conforms very closely to the standards set out by the Committee of Council on Education in their memorandum of 1851. The plan (Fig. 8) consists of a main schoolroom, with a small classroom opening off it. Both rooms have galleries at one end. The interior of the master's house consists of sitting-room, kitchen, scullery, and three bedrooms.

Ironbridge National School [Church of England] (Plate 28), dated 1859, is built of blue brick and ashlar dressings, and stands on the south side of St. Luke's Road. The architect and contractor was Samuel Nevett of Ironbridge[47] and the cost about £1,800.[48]

The design is Tudor Gothic and the front faces south. This has a central bell-tower, lacking the original upper stage, flanked at either end by projecting gable wings. Some windows are mullioned and transomed, generally with lattice glazing. The master's house forms part of the total design and lies at the east end.

The internal layout (Fig. 8) again conforms to the arrangements recommended by the Committee of Council in the 1851 Memorandum. The schoolroom is oblong with groups of desks arranged along one wall. Each group is separated from the group next to it by an alley, along which a curtain could be drawn. A small classroom with a gallery opens off the main schoolroom.

The **Coalbrookdale Literary and Scientific Institution** (Plate 29 and Fig. 9) was financed and built by the Coalbrookdale Company as an adult education centre for its employees. It is built of blue and white brick, produced at the company's works, and the architect was the works manager, Charles Crookes. The building was opened on 30 May 1859.[49]

Fig. 9   Original front of Coalbrookdale Literary and Scientific Institute (1859)

The original design (Fig. 9) is conventional Tudor Gothic. The ornamental curved gables have been removed, together with the original entablature on which the words 'Literary and Scientific Institution' were inscribed in moulded brick.

21

The principal elevation is of seven bays, with brick hood-moulds to the transomed windows, and white brick quoins. Attached to the north end is a small residence for the librarian.

The interior originally comprised a lecture hall with gallery, a library, reading room, art room and smaller ancillary rooms. The building was lit by gas and warmed by central heating.

Farm Buildings

Local conditions, encouraged investment in farm buildings. The growth of industry in the surrounding area assured a large local market for farm products, and provided a source of income for ironmasters. Abraham Darby III worked three farms, at Madeley, Sunniside, and the Hay, and invested considerable sums on their improvement.[50] These local farms were able to supply the large number of horses needed to provide power and transport for the works, mines, roads, and canals. This demand was an inducement to create extensive stabling at the farms, and facilities for storing oats for fodder.

Sunniside farm has been demolished, but a complete range of agricultural buildings stands a short distance from the **Hay House, Madeley** (Fig. 10). The group dates in its basic shape and form from the 18th century, and consists of a courtyard, with three outlying buildings. The courtyard group is typical of its period in that each building was originally detached from its neighbours and the corners of the courtyard open. It consists of two barns, a cowhouse, stable, granary, and covered yard.

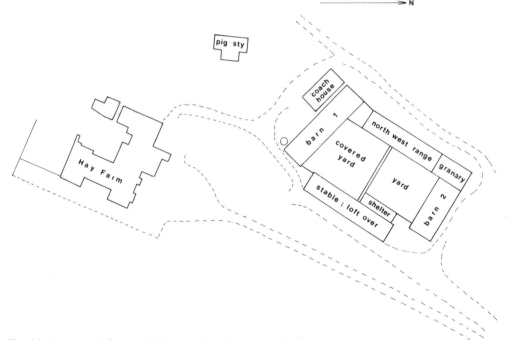

Fig. 10   Layout of farm buildings at The Hay Farm, Madeley

The oldest barn dates from the 17th century and is of stone. It is of five unequal bays, with a central threshing-floor. The gables were originally timber-framed. At the south-west corner is the remains of a 19th-century horse engine track. The second barn is later, dating from the mid-18th century, and is of brick and stone. It is of five bays and has a central threshing-floor. The internal roof trusses are of two types: king-posts, with queen-posts adjoining the threshing-floor. The cowhouse is probably older and is notable for the height of its loft, 3.6m. (12ft.). The loft wall is thickened on the inner side of the quadrangle to contain 13 rows of nest holes, which form an unusually large linear dovecote containing over five hundred nests.

The stable, dated 1775, is the largest single building on the farmstead, and the front elevation is 27.7m. (90.7ft.) long. The upper storey contains a series of brick ventilation openings to the loft (Plate 30), and louvre-windows to the ground-floor stables (Plate 31). The interior stalls each have an upper rack and wooden manger resting on an arched recess (Plate 32).[51] At the back of the stable is a very early example of a continuous lean-to shelter shed. Half of the yard was covered over in the late 19th century by a large twin-span roof.[52] To the north of this courtyard group is a cartshed, and to the south a three-bay pigsty with henloft over.

A more modest range of farm buildings survives at **The Lees**, Coalport Road (Plate 33). This comprises a detached barn, stable block a group of ancillary buildings to the north, including a brewhouse, dairy and granary.

Chapter Four

DOMESTIC BUILDINGS

The Severn Gorge is rich in surviving examples of distinctive types of domestic buildings. These dwellings were built for different status groups, ranging from those intended for the minor gentry, factory owners, and the professional classes, to those erected for tradesmen and industrial workers. Thus there is a wide variety of domestic architecture, from relatively modest country mansions to smaller cottages, farmhouses and terraced rows of industrial housing.

A number of these domestic buildings survive intact, but many have been altered over the years. In the 18th and 19th centuries it was common to sub-divide large houses into separate tenements, and several buildings were altered in this way, and are now under multiple occupation.[53] In recent years many of the smaller houses and cottages have been extensively modernised, and in some cases one is left with only the shell of the original building. There has also been a growing tendency to alter exteriors, for example, to replace the traditional forms of window glazing with modern factory-made substitutes. Despite all these changes, the buildings have survived relatively untouched until recently, and they have not been destroyed by the process of urban renewal that has affected so many British cities.

In this section domestic buildings are grouped into two main categories. A distinction is made between what may be loosely described as 'polite' architecture on the one hand, and 'vernacular' architecture on the other.[54] The term polite architecture is used to describe a building designed by a professional architect or surveyor, according to contemporary national or even international fashion, in which great emphasis is placed on aesthetic considerations. Vernacular architecture, in contrast, refers to buildings designed by an amateur craftsman or builder, following local building practices, to build traditional houses in which functional design is dominant.

In practice, the distinction between the two types is one of degree, and most buildings fall between the two extremes of either wholly polite or wholly vernacular, possessing some vernacular and some polite content. The terraces of company housing in Coalbrookdale are a case in point. These rows were designed and planned according to a carefully predetermined layout, probably by a surveyor. The idea of building houses in continuous terraced rows of this type is an innovation in local domestic architecture and is not traditional. Yet some of the constructional details of the terraces, for example, the mullion and transom windows with segmental brick arches, are indigenous vernacular features

24

not derived from polite architecture. Thus the terraces are something of a hybrid design. But clearly the fashionable large houses on Darby Road, for instance, with their imposing façades, are examples of polite architecture, whilst the numerous small cottages that form the bulk of the building in the Gorge are vernacular in quality.

House Elevations

The oldest surviving building in the Severn Gorge, The Lodge at Ironbridge (Plate 34), dates from the mid-16th century, and was possibly built as a hunting lodge or observation tower for the nearby manor house of Madeley Court.[55] The principal front consists of a two-and-a-half-storey tower built of large, coursed stone blocks, and in the upper part of the south and west gables are small circular unglazed window openings.

Large detached mansion houses are few in number and date from the 17th century. Two call for mention. The Tuckies House, Jackfield (Plate 35) has an approximately symmetrical front, with slightly projecting wings and hipped dormers. The west wing is the oldest, the east wing being added when the house was remodelled in the 18th century. Of about the same date is the Hay House, Madeley, on the opposite bank of the river. Again, it has a roughly symmetrical front with projecting wings. These have hipped gables, and the south wing is the older. This house was re-fronted in the 18th century, when the north wing was added.

The stone and timber-framed vernacular cottages built before 1700 are not generally constructed with symmetrical fronts. The best surviving range, at Nos. 4–7 Dale Road, Coalbrookdale (Plate 36), dated 1636, is a modest group of one-and-a-half-storey cottages with four gabled dormers, but no attempt is made at symmetry in the placing of doors and window openings.

The elevations of houses built between 1700 and 1820 can be considered in five main groups.

(1) **Large detached residences** built for the wealthy servant-keeping class.These begin to appear in numbers from the mid-18th century. They are houses of some distinction, conforming very closely to prevalent architectural taste. The fashionable brick fronts are well proportioned and symmetrical, with a central doorcase, sash windows in flush frames, and occasionally stone dressings on the better houses. Typical groups of these residences were erected in Darby Road, Coalbrookdale, from the mid-18th century. The best frontage, the Grange (Plate 37) is symmetrical and of five bays. The entrance has an arched window light, and the door-case a pediment supported on slender console brackets. The front is of brick with stone quoins. The windows are sashes set in flush frames and the flat window arches are of rubbed brick with projecting stone keyblocks.

The other large residences in Darby Road include Dale House, now drastically altered, Nos. 10 and 29, The Chestnuts, and the nearby Green Bank Farm House. The largest detached house, Sunniside, dating from the mid-18th century, has been demolished. Elsewhere in the Severn Gorge, three houses are worthy of mention: The Calcutts House, Jackfield (Plate 38), a fine three-bay front dating from *c.* 1755; Belmont House, Ironbridge (Plate 39), a broader five-bay elevation, dated 1753, and Severn House, Coalbrookdale (the *Valley* hotel) now much altered and converted into an hotel.

(2) **Double-fronted Houses** begin to appear in numbers after 1750. They are generally built on small separate plots of land, each with a front garden. The early fronts are one-and-a-half storeys in height, and sometimes the entrance door is placed off-centre, as at No. 54 New Bridge Road, Ironbridge (Plate 40). Later examples, such as No. 1 St. Luke's Road, Ironbridge (Plate 41), have a central entrance and are fully two storeys in height. Architectural elaboration of the front is uncommon. One of the few instances occurs at Primrose Cottage, Coalbrookdale (Plate 42), where the windows have pointed arches with Y-shaped tracery.

In the final quarter of the 18th century, increasing importance is given to the principal elevation of the double-fronted house. Sashes replace mullion and transom windows as the normal type, and a variety of new lintels are used. These lintels are made of cast-iron or artificial stone, and are usually used with matching sills. Greater prominence is given to the entrance by incorporating a door-case, together with a six-panelled door (Plate 43), and fronts become generally more impressive.

(3) **Cottages build in pairs** are common in the Gorge. The earliest examples, as at Nos. 34–5 Belmont Road, date from the 17th century. A small pair of early brick cottages survives in a semi-derelict state at Nos. 14–15 Woodlands Road, Ironbridge (Plate 44), but other examples, including a notable group at Dale End, Coalbrookdale (Plate 45) have been demolished.[56]

Paired cottages frequently form part of a symmetrical architectural composition, as at Nos. 15–16 Church Hill, Ironbridge (Fig. 14). A balanced façade is achieved by placing both entrance doors in the centre with windows at either side and the effect is to produce a cottage which has the superficial appearance of a double-fronted house. In fact, many of these cottages have been knocked together and one entrance bricked up, to convert them into double-fronted houses of this type (Plate 46 shows an example in Jackfield).

(4) **Single-fronted Cottages** occur in large numbers throughout the district. The earliest fronts are one-and-a-half storeys in height with prominent dormer windows breaking into the main roof space (Plate 46). Frequently they were built next to each other, or adjoining a small house. Where they were built in groups they often have a common frontage and roof line, but breaks in the wall face sometimes indicate that they have been constructed separately, as in the case with Nos. 44–47 (Plate 47), and Nos. 52–54 (Plate 48), Wellington Road, Coalbrookdale.

Elevations are generally very plain. The early 18th-century fronts occasionally have brick string-courses and gable parapets, but other forms of decoration are sparse. Later, window heads of flat brick or small door canopies occurred. By 1800 the single-fronted cottage was fully two storeys in height, and the earlier one-and-a-half and two-and-a-half storey types had fallen out of general use.

26

(5) **Rows of Terraced Housing** were built in Coalbrookdale from the second quarter of the 18th century. These are discussed in greater detail later. A good example of a 19th-century terrace occurs in Ironbridge at Nos. 2–6 New Road (Plate 49). The elevation of this row of five cottages is distinguished by the use of wooden door-cases, stone lintels, and sash windows.

Post-1820 elevations show increasing variety, as the last remnants of the vernacular tradition gradually disappeared. In the second quarter of the century a number of larger detached houses were built, including several on Church Hill, Ironbridge. The traditional Classical style remained popular and fronts are generally symmetrical with an elaborate door-case between sash windows, as at No. 8 New Road, Ironbridge (Plate 50). Another impressive front is at South View, Ironbridge (Plate 51), but in this instance part of the symmetry of the original design has been lost through the addition of an extra bay in the 19th century.

Detached villas in the Gothic style were built from *c.* 1840 onwards, and were designed according to picturesque taste, symmetry being studiously avoided. The Orchard, Ironbridge, was built *c.*1843,[57] and later another villa at No. 10 Madeley Road. After 1850 some elevations incorporated Italianate features.

Use of Rooms

The downstairs **living-room** is a standard feature of all vernacular cottages. It provided the main living area, and was usually heated by the principal fireplace which generally contained a range for cooking (Plate 52). After *c.* 1770 it became common to add a **parlour**, a smaller room apart from the living-room which gave a subsidiary space that could be used for entertaining visitors. The parlour was generally given a more elaborate architectural treatment than the living-room. The floor, for instance, might be boarded rather than of brick, and the fireplace might have an elaborate mantel. In one case a wall of the parlour is panelled (Plate 53).

The **back-kitchen** was first widely introduced in the 18th century. Thenceforth cooking could be transferred from the front living-room into a separate kitchen at the back of the house. A back-kitchen usually contained a cottage range, and perhaps a bread oven.

A **scullery** was often attached to a back-kitchen, and this extra room provided additional accommodation where dishes could be washed, and kitchen utensils and food stored. A setlas (Plate 54), a flat-tiled working surface supported on brick arches, was frequently built against the side wall of a scullery or back-kitchen. A few houses had a separate **pantry** or larder in which provisions were kept.

Most cottages had access to a **brewhouse** (Fig. 11), usually a separate outbuilding nearby. Normally the brewhouse was communal and shared with a neighbour. It contained a cast-iron boiler, heated by a small grate, for washing clothes, and sometimes a setlas. Brewhouses were used traditionally for brewing ale, or for hanging a freshly-killed pig before it was dressed.[58] Among the other outbuildings there was usually an **earth-closet**, with an ash pit nearby, and also a separate **coal-house**.

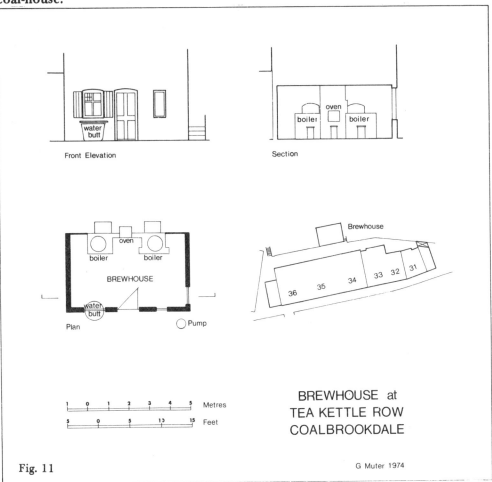

Front Elevation

Section

oven

boiler | boiler

oven

boiler | boiler

BREWHOUSE

water butt

Plan

Pump

Brewhouse

36 35 34 33 32 31

```
1   0   1   2   3   4   5   Metres
5   0   5   10  15  Feet
```

BREWHOUSE at
TEA KETTLE ROW
COALBROOKDALE

Fig. 11

G Muter 1974

Larger buildings had more rooms and a better standard of accommodation. The larger 18th-century houses sometimes had a **saloon** on the first floor, which formed the principal room overlooking the street or roadway. In the 19th century there were a variety of different plan types amongst the larger houses. A description of accommodation at South View (formerly Lincoln Hill House), built *c.* 1830, lists the following rooms:[59] in the basement a cellar; on the ground floor an entrance hall, dining-room, drawing-room, kitchens and pantry; on the first floor three chambers and bathroom; on the second floor three chambers; also a conservatory, stable, coach-house, and outbuildings.

Vernacular House Plan Types

So few houses dating from the period before 1700 survive that it is not possible to trace any development in internal layout and design prior to this date. But after 1700, as the number of surviving buildings increases, a pattern does become discernible. The tendency is, as time progresses, for buildings to increase in size and expand the number of rooms in general use. The oldest houses are often small with only a single downstairs living-room, but later space standards are greatly improved and it is common to find vernacular houses with two, three, or even four ground-floor rooms by 1830.[60]

The **Single-Unit** plan was the most common early type and continued in use until the late 17th century. In this plan the living accommodation consisted of a single room on the ground floor which formed the principal living area. This room was generally heated by a large hearth on which the cooking was done. The entire area of the first floor was usually given over to form a partitioned sleeping chamber, which was generally approached by a steep narrow staircase of winders. Some cottages possessed small cellars, usually accessible from the outside gable wall, and frequently a pantry or small wash-house was built on to the back as a separate lean-to.

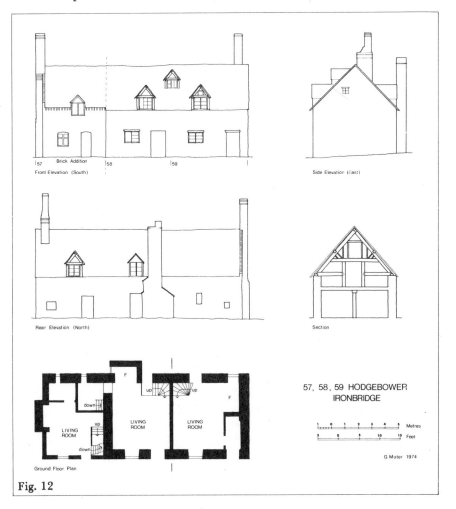

57, 58, 59 HODGEBOWER
IRONBRIDGE

G Muter 1974

Fig. 12

29

A plan of this type (Plate 55 and Fig. 12) shows the internal layout of a modest pair of 16th-century stone cottages, Nos. 58–59 Hodgebower, Ironbridge. Here the accommodation is of the simplest type, and the ground-floor living area consists of a single room only, heated by a large side-hearth. The staircases of both cottages wind up against a sturdy, central, timber-framed partition, and lead to two small bedroom chambers on the first floor, and above this to a small garret in the loft.

The **Two-Unit** plan was a more highly developed type, widely in use in the 18th century. This plan comprised two ground-floor rooms, a living-room and either a parlour or a back-kitchen. In the earliest examples, it was common to place the living-room at the front, and the back-kitchen or scullery in a wing at the back. The stair usually ran up against the back wall of the living-room.

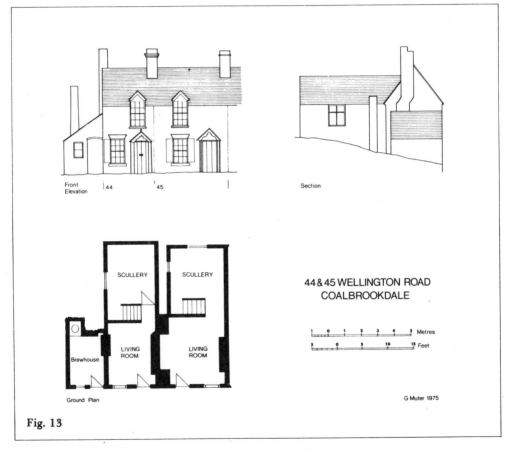

Fig. 13

Some of these two-unit houses were originally single-unit dwellings that had an extra room added sometime in the 18th century. There are several instances of this in Coalbrookdale. Figure 13 illustrates two cottages, Nos. 44–45 Wellington Road, both altered in this way. The original plan had a single front living-room, but later a back-kitchen was added beneath a gabled extension at the rear.

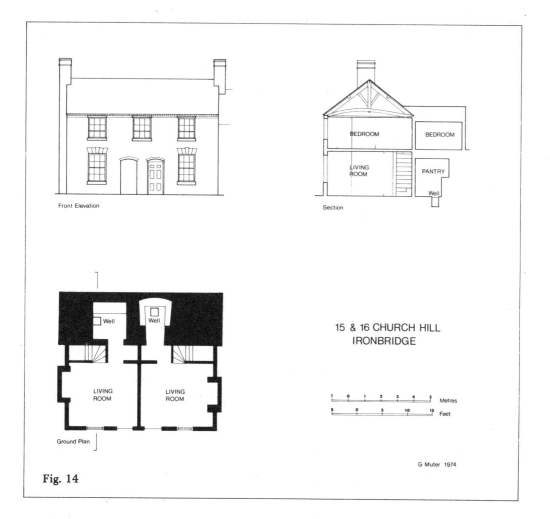

Front Elevation

Section

BEDROOM

BEDROOM

LIVING
ROOM

PANTRY

Well

Well

Well

LIVING
ROOM

LIVING
ROOM

Ground Plan

15 & 16 CHURCH HILL
IRONBRIDGE

1 0 1 2 3 4 5 Metres

5 0 5 10 15 Feet

G Muter 1974

Fig. 14

Figure 14 illustrates another variation of the two-unit plan. The diagram shows a pair of cottages, Nos. 15–16 Church Hill, Ironbridge. Each cottage had a living-room at the front, and a small pantry in a recess at the rear. These rear pantries were not added but were part of the original design, and they contain small wells for the supply of domestic water.[61] The design probably dates from *c.* 1780.

Yet another variation of the two-unit plan originated at about the same time. Instead of placing the two ground-floor rooms one behind the other, it became common to turn the design on its side, so that both rooms were placed next to one another at the front of the house. Thus the living-room and parlour were built beside each other in a line. One of the attractions of this arrangement was that it permitted a symmetrical treatment of the houe front. This balance was achieved by placing the entrance doorway in the centre and windows on either side, thus creating the standard double-fronted small house.

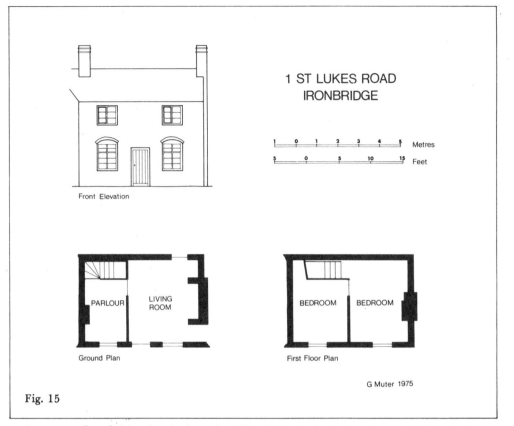

1 ST LUKES ROAD
IRONBRIDGE

Metres

Feet

Front Elevation

PARLOUR | LIVING ROOM

Ground Plan

BEDROOM | BEDROOM

First Floor Plan

G Muter 1975

Fig. 15

An example of this plan is found at No. 1 St. Luke's Road, Ironbridge (Plate 41 and Fig. 15). The layout shows two rooms on the ground floor, a living-room to the right, and a smaller parlour opening off it to the left. Each room is heated by a fireplace in the gable wall. There is no entrance lobby, and the front door opens directly into the living-room, with the staircase placed at the back of the parlour.

The **Three-Unit** plan was a common late 18th-century type and many houses were constructed to this design. It was normal for the living-room and parlour to be placed next to each other, as in the contemporary two-unit design, with an additional service-room in a wing at the back. An instance of this layout occurs at No. 8 Darby Road, Coalbrookdale (Fig. 16), where there is a back-kitchen behind the living-room at the rear of the house, giving a total of three rooms on the ground floor. This layout represents a significant improvement in accommodation and space standards.

The **Four-Unit** plan was a further development of the three-unit type, achieved by building two rear service-rooms instead of just one. Figure 17 illustrates the arrangement in one particular case, at No. 30 Wellington Road, Coalbrookdale. The design comprises a living-room and parlour at the front, and a back-kitchen plus a pantry/cold store at the rear. This type of house is the local equivalent of the double-pile or double-depth house. Whereas houses of this plan in other parts of England are often roofed in single (or two parallel) spans,[62] the standard local design is to incorporate the service rooms under two short wings projecting at right-angles from the back of one long span roof.

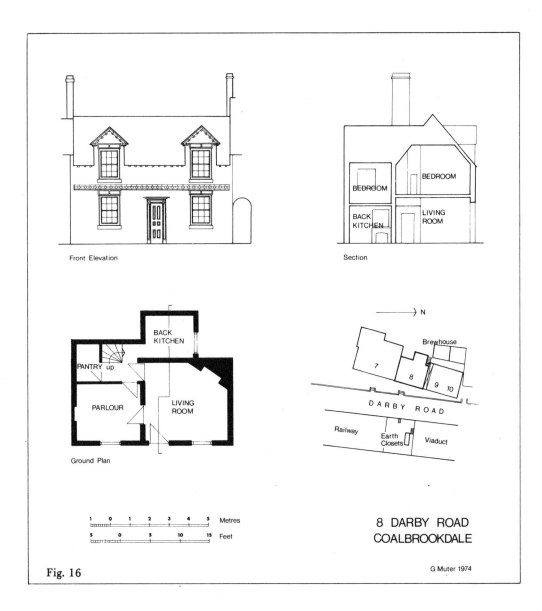

Front Elevation

Section

BEDROOM

BEDROOM

BACK KITCHEN

LIVING ROOM

BACK KITCHEN

PANTRY up

PARLOUR

LIVING ROOM

Ground Plan

N

Brewhouse

7

8

9   10

D A R B Y   R O A D

Railway

Earth Closets

Viaduct

1 0 1 2 3 4 5   Metres

5 0 5 10 15   Feet

8 DARBY ROAD
COALBROOKDALE

Fig. 16

G Muter 1974

Front Elevation

Side Elevation

COLD STORE

BACK KITCHEN

PANTRY

PARLOUR

LIVING ROOM

up

Ground Plan

BEDROOM

down

BEDROOM

BEDROOM

First Floor Plan

Church Road

Wellington Road

29

30

Earth Closet

N

30 WELLINGTON ROAD
COALBROOKDALE

1 0 1 2 3 4 5   Metres

5 0 5 10 15   Feet

G Muter 1974

Fig. 17

34

Chapter Five

TERRACED HOUSING IN THE COALBROOKDALE VALLEY

The oldest range of terraced houses in Coalbrookdale was **Nailor's Row** (Nos. 38–47 The Wharfage) (Plate 56), a long range of brick houses which formerly abutted and stretched westwards from the Severn Wharf Building (Fig. 18).

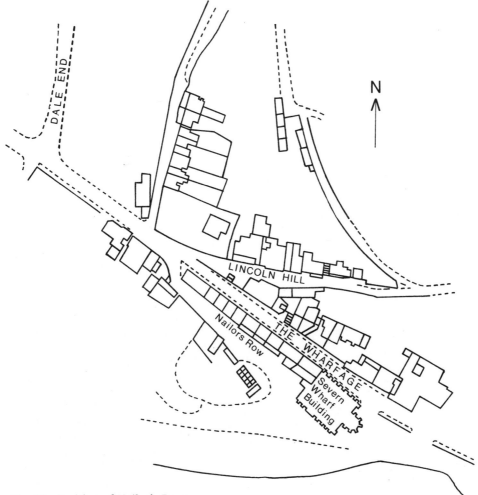

Fig. 18 Position of Nailor's Row

Some buildings in the row were two-storey, others had attics as an additional half-storey. The row, now demolished, had mullion and transom windows in cambered head openings, and plain doors.[63] The terrace was first leased to the Coalbrookdale Company on 20 March 1733, but it was probably altered and repaired in 1794.[64]

In the 1740s another terrace of houses was built in Darby Road, Coalbrookdale, and this came to be known as **Tea Kettle Row** (Nos. 31–36 Darby Road) (Plate 57 and Fig. 19). There is no evidence to suggest that this row was built by the Coalbrookdale Company, and it predates the later Coalbrookdale rows by some forty years, being built to an entirely different design.

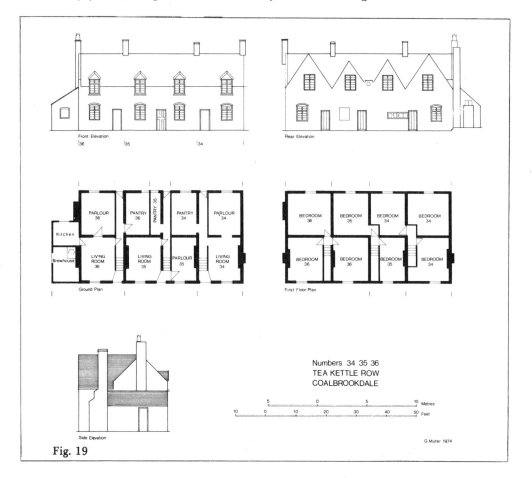

Fig. 19

Tea Kettle Row was built in three separate stages. Breaks in the external wall face and differences in internal planning confirm this. But the elevation has unity and consists of a continuous range of six one-and-a-half-storey dwellings with a common roof line. A number of external features recur throughout the row, including mullion and transom windows, segmental arched window heads, gabled dormers, brick string-courses, and projecting rafters at the eaves.

The plan of part of this row, a group of houses (Nos. 34–36 Darby Road) at its southern end, is illustrated in Fig. 19. The layout is an exceedingly complex design, with the three houses interlocking and overlapping with one another on both floors. During restoration of No. 34 in 1974 an inscription dated 6 December 1746 was revealed on an upstairs wall.[65]

Each of the three houses has a living-room, a parlour, and a pantry on the ground floor, but the position varies. In the two end houses (Nos. 34 and 36), the living-room is placed at the front, with the parlour in a wing at the back. But in the central house (No. 35) the living-room and the parlour are both placed at the front, and the accommodation at the back provides space for three small pantries. There are further variations on the first floor where the houses are built over each other in places. A bedroom of No. 36, for example, is placed over the living-room of No. 35, and a bedroom of No. 35 is placed above pantries of Nos. 35 and 36. This is a complex and very ingenious design, providing more spacious accommodation than the later Coalbrookdale Company rows.

It was not until the fourth quarter of the 18th century that the Coalbrookdale Company built terraces of industrial housing in the valley. These company rows are among the earliest industrial terraces in Great Britain, and are a particularly significant group of buildings in the Severn Gorge.

Situated in what was then a comparatively remote rural part of Shropshire, close to all the natural resources for iron-making, but far away from established centres of population, the Coalbrookdale ironfounders, like factory owners elsewhere,[66] were faced with the problem of attracting employees to settle in the area. One way of achieving this was the creation of terraces of industrial housing. These were built and managed by the ironworks to provide accommodation for its workpeople. In this way the Coalbrookdale Company came to provide housing for its employees: its role was similar to that of the 18th-century country landowner who built cottages to house his estate workers. It was an enlightened expedient.

The building of company houses not only provided much-needed housing for workers, but also made sound economic sense. Tenemented property was a recognised form of capital investment in the late 18th century. Returns were generally lower than could be obtained in manufacturing industry, but investment in housing was less of a risk and had the advantage of yielding a constant return of between 7 and 12 per cent. gross.[67]

The Coalbrookdale Company charged a rental of 7½ per cent. on its property in the early 1790s.[68] This was not by any means an extortionate figure, but something higher than the philanthropy at 5 per cent. that became fashionable in the mid-19th century.[69] Certainly a 7½ per cent. yield would have provided the company with an adequate return on the capital employed, and even made housing a profitable investment. Thus company housing was not solely an act of industrial paternalism; there was an element of self-interest.

This is illustrated in a particular example for which figures are available. Carpenter's Row (Plate 58), a terrace of eight cottages, probably built shortly after 1783, was sold during the trade recession of 1794 for £220.[70] The rental from the row was then £16 16s. 0d. per year.[71] This rate gave a respectable yield on the investment of slightly over 7½ per cent. gross. The cost of each house worked out at roughly £28 per dwelling, and the rental was fixed at about 9½d. per week.

The five company rows in Coalbrookdale cannot be dated with exact certainty. Documentary evidence is fragmentary. The land on which Carpenter's Row stands was originally assigned to the Coalbrookdale Company on 22 March 1783,[72] and construction of the row probably started soon afterwards. Charity Row is shown in a pencil sketch by Joseph Farington, dated 1789.[73] The other rows were certainly up by 1794, when they appear on a lease map.[74]

The Coalbrookdale Company was at its zenith after 1780. The rapid expansion of the works in the decade between 1770–1780 had made it possibly the largest iron foundry in Great Britain. This upsurge in manufacturing activity and the consequent pressure for expansion must have provided both the impetus and the capital for a fairly large-scale company house-building programme, probably between about 1780–1793.

The standard company house in Coalbrookdale was a two-room dwelling, two storeys high, laid out in medium-sized terraces of up to 10 units. The layout was designed to an L-plan, composed of two rooms: a main living-room which was roughly square, and a small pantry leading off it, at one side. A steep narrow stair climbed from the living-room to a partitioned sleeping chamber which extended over the whole of the upper floor. Each living-room had a substantial fireplace and a floor-covering of tile squares or brick paviours. Sanitation originally consisted of small groups of privies situated near each terrace.

Each terrace was a mixture of alternately single-fronted and double-fronted houses. This unusual arrangement arose from the internal layout. In the double-fronted houses the pantry was placed at the front, with a small bedroom above, while in the single-fronted cottages the pantry was located at the rear. These interlocking pantries were a characteristic feature of all company terraces in Coalbrookdale.

External construction was of brick and tile. The outer walls were of 240mm. (9½in.) brickwork, laid in Flemish stretcher bond. The ground-floor window openings were spanned by segmental arches of brick headers[75] and had no sills. Windows were double-light transoms made to a standard size measuring approximately 1.40m. (4ft. 7in.) by 1.02m. (3ft. 4in.). Pantry windows were usually half this size, and the first-floor windows were smaller, and had no transom. Double-light windows had a single opening casement in most cases. Original doors were ledged and battened. Roofs were constructed of standard-sized tiles laid in regular even courses, and chimneys had cast-iron 'pots'.

The map (Fig. 20) shows the location of the five terraces built to this pattern in Coalbrookdale between c. 1780 and 1793. The minor variations and distinguishing features of these individual terraces are described next.

School House Row (Fig. 21), also known as Rookery Row and Chapel Row, consisted of 10 houses in one terrace measuring 55.2m. (181ft.). The block is no longer standing, but the illustration (Fig. 21) is a reconstruction drawn from field measurements made prior to its demolition in 1960.[76] The brewhouses in this row were built inside the terrace at either end, and the space above provided

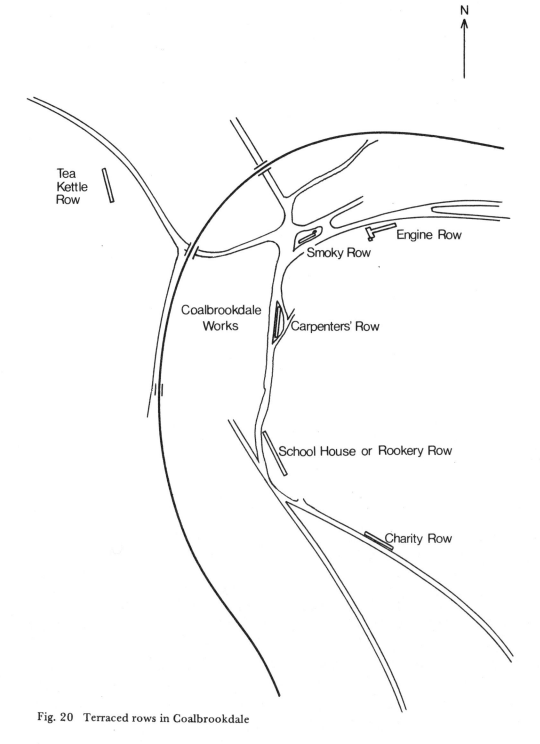

N

Tea
Kettle
Row

Engine Row

Smoky Row

Coalbrookdale
Works

Carpenters' Row

School House or Rookery Row

Charity Row

Fig. 20   Terraced rows in Coalbrookdale

an extra bedroom for each end house. Living-rooms had corner fireplaces[77] with the flues brought together to form coupled chimneys at the back. There had been alterations to the row. Sculleries had been added to the rear and one of the centre living-rooms had been converted into a brewhouse. In some instances the staircase had been moved from the living-room into the pantry. None of the houses originally had back doors.

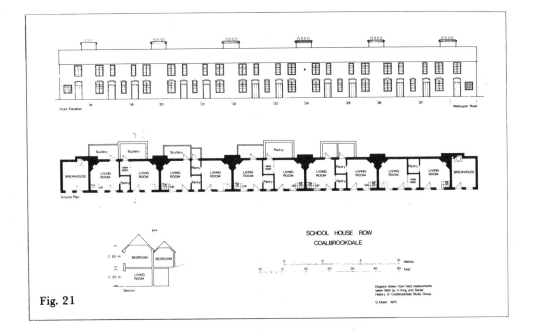

Fig. 21

SCHOOL HOUSE ROW
COALBROOKDALE

Carpenters' Row (Plate 58 and Fig. 22), probably built shortly after 1783, is still standing, although many houses are empty and semi-derelict. It consists of eight houses in a single row measuring 41.4m. (135.8ft.). the layout is similar to that of School House Row in that the brewhouses are built inside the main block at the ends of the building, and the living-rooms have corner fireplaces. Pantry windows are single-light transoms, half the size of living-room windows. Yet the design of the terrace is symmetrical, and Nos. 1–5 are exact mirror-images of Nos. 6–10. The original appearance of the block has been altered by later additions at the back.

40

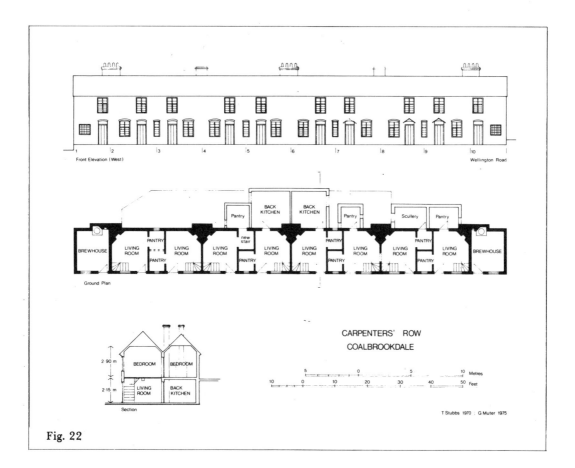

Front Elevation (West)

Wellington Road

BREWHOUSE LIVING ROOM PANTRY LIVING ROOM LIVING ROOM Pantry BACK KITCHEN BACK KITCHEN new stair LIVING ROOM LIVING ROOM PANTRY PANTRY Pantry LIVING ROOM LIVING ROOM Scullery PANTRY Pantry PANTRY LIVING ROOM BREWHOUSE PANTRY

Ground Plan

BEDROOM BEDROOM 2·90 m LIVING ROOM BACK KITCHEN 2·15 m

Section

CARPENTERS' ROW
COALBROOKDALE

5   0   5   10 Metres
10   0   10   20   30   40   50 Feet

T Stubbs 1970 : G Muter 1975

Fig. 22

Engine Row (Plate 59) consists of six houses, built in two blocks, of four and two dwellings. The larger block surveyed in 1974 (Fig. 23) is still partly occupied, though portions are empty and semi-derelict. The row is said to take its name from the steam engine 'Resolution' constructed by the Coalbrookdale Company on adjacent ground during 1781–1783.[78] The brewhouse in the main block originally occupied the end room on the ground floor. This was later converted into a living-room and a new brewhouse built on to the end of the row. There have been other internal alterations, but the characteristic L-plan is clearly discernible. The pantry windows in this row are double-light transoms, equal in size to those of the living-room. This gives a uniform emphasis to each bay of the front elevation. The upper windows are replacements.

41

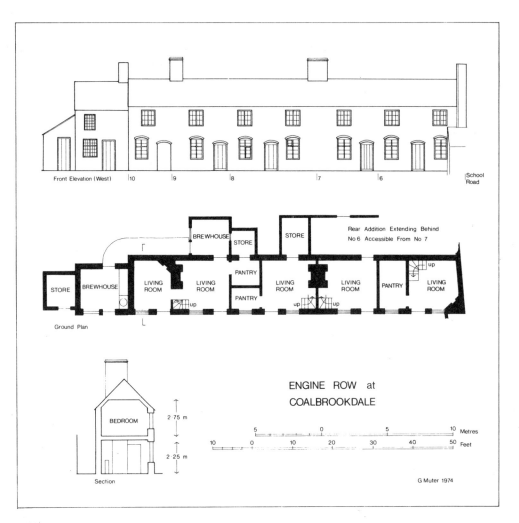

Front Elevation (West)　｜10　｜9　｜8　｜7　｜6　｜School Road

BREWHOUSE　STORE　STORE　Rear Addition Extending Behind No 6 Accessible From No 7

PANTRY

STORE　BREWHOUSE　LIVING ROOM　LIVING ROOM　PANTRY　LIVING ROOM　LIVING ROOM　PANTRY　LIVING ROOM　up

up　up　up

Ground Plan

BEDROOM　2·75 m

2·25 m

Section

ENGINE ROW at COALBROOKDALE

5　0　5　10　Metres

10　0　10　20　30　40　50　Feet

G Muter 1974

Fig. 23

Charity Row consists of six houses in a single block, measuring 34.2m. (112.2ft.). The row is still standing, but the exterior has been partly rendered and many windows replaced. Fig. 24 shows the original external appearance and the existing interior layout. The row is distinguished from the other company terraces in Coalbrookdale by the brewhouse being located away from the main block in a separate outbuilding. The position of the fireplaces is also different, being placed in the centre wall of the living-room, instead of across one corner. Unlike the other company rows, the terrace has a back alley with privies opening off it and each house has a back door. Traditionally, the row is believed to have been built by the Coalbrookdale Company to accommodate the widows of former employees.[79]

42

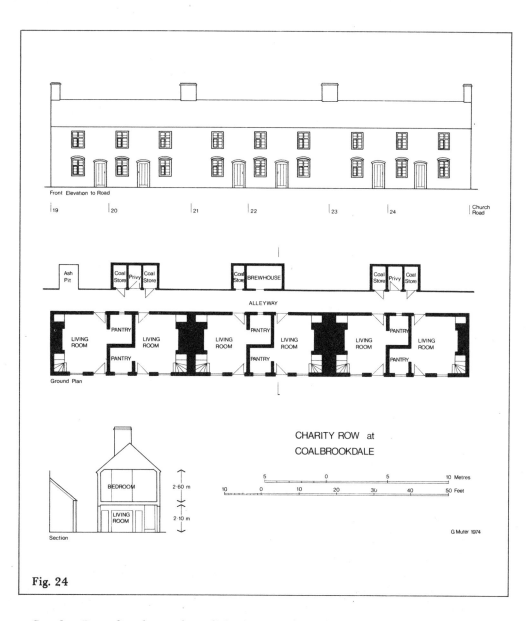

Front Elevation to Road

| 19 | 20 | 21 | 22 | 23 | 24 | Church Road

Ash Pit

Coal Store | Privy | Coal Store | Coal Store | BREWHOUSE | Coal Store | Privy | Coal Store

ALLEYWAY

PANTRY | PANTRY | PANTRY | PANTRY

LIVING ROOM | LIVING ROOM | LIVING ROOM | LIVING ROOM | LIVING ROOM | LIVING ROOM

PANTRY | PANTRY | PANTRY | PANTRY

Ground Plan

CHARITY ROW at
COALBROOKDALE

BEDROOM

2·60 m

LIVING ROOM

2·10 m

Section

5   0   5   10 Metres
10 0 10 20 30 40 50 Feet

G Muter 1974

Fig. 24

Smoky Row has been demolished. It consisted of four houses and one brew-house, but there is uncertainty about its internal layout and design.[80]

The Census Enumerator's Returns of 1851 give a clear picture of the occupancy of the terraces in Coalbrookdale some sixty years after they were built.[81] The occupancy varied widely, from eight persons per dwelling down to one. Figures were least for Charity Row, which had an average of two occupants per house. Five houses had seven or more occupants, and must have been overcrowded, even by the standards of the time. Fig. 25 shows that most

43

of the working inhabitants were engaged in skilled and semi-skilled tasks. The occupations of moulder and fitter were well represented, but there were comparatively few labourers. The data confirms the view that Charity Row, as

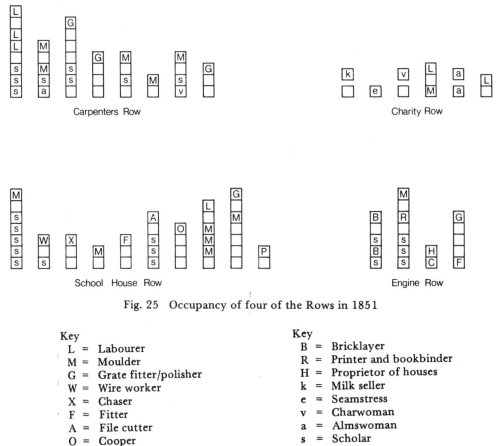

Fig. 25 Occupancy of four of the Rows in 1851

Key
L = Labourer
M = Moulder
G = Grate fitter/polisher
W = Wire worker
X = Chaser
F = Fitter
A = File cutter
O = Cooper
P = Painter

Key
B = Bricklayer
R = Printer and bookbinder
H = Proprietor of houses
k = Milk seller
e = Seamstress
v = Charwoman
a = Almswoman
s = Scholar

its name suggests, housed the widows of former employees; there were two almswomen, a seamstress, a charwoman, and a milk-seller in residence.

The dimensions of each house gave reasonably adequate space standards. The floor area averaged almost 33 sq. m. Headroom was moderately good. Certainly the rows represented a higher standard of accommodation than was being built in parts of Wales at a roughly contemporary date.[82] The company houses in Coalbrookdale were small, compact dwellings, comparatively well-built, with adequate ventilation, and provided enough space for food storage and preparation.

Four rows—School House Row, Carpenters' Row, Engine Row, and Charity Row—housed a total of 110 occupants in 1851. If Smoky Row is included the total is higher. Even so, the figure must represent only a fraction of the total number of employees at the Coalbrookdale works in 1851. No figures are available for the 1780s, but again it is likely that the terraces housed only a

44

proportion of the workforce; it is interesting to speculate where the remainder of them lived. Did they travel into the valley daily from the surrounding towns of Madeley, Broseley and Wellington? Or did they live in nearby squatter settlements?[83] Is it possible that some lived in hovels constructed of such impermanent materials that they have now altogether disappeared?[84] These are important questions that remain unanswered.[85]

Chapter Six

MATERIALS AND CONSTRUCTION

Materials

Timber-Framing is the most common structural material in use before 1700. Few timber-framed buildings have survived, and the most impressive example, The Lloyds House, Coalport (dated 1621) has been destroyed.[86]

Evidence of only one cruck house has been discovered. The remains of this were formerly visible in the gable wall of No. 23 High Street, Ironbridge, following the demolition of an adjacent group of buildings in 1969. It was an upper cruck consisting of a pair of curved blades with a 20ft. span.[87]

The most common structural type of timber-framing is post-and-truss construction. The framing is generally simple and it is unusual for houses to be jettied. Walls are framed in a grid of plain studs, intermediate rails and occasionally struts in the gable wall. The spacing of studs varies between buildings, some being noticeably closer together than others. Timbers generally have a good scantling and are not skimped or flimsy.

The infilling of the framing is generally of wattle and daub (Plate 60), but in some examples bricks are used. Few timber-framed buildings have survived intact. Some, like Yew Tree Cottage, Coalbrookdale, have been heavily restored. Others have had the principal elevation obscured by a brick casing or rough-cast, as at No. 69 Bower Yard, Ironbridge.

External detail is very sparse. Wall surfaces are generally made up of a grid of square-shaped panels. These are plain, lacking any of the decorative enrichments common, for example, in Lancashire or Cheshire.[88] Elaboration is minimal, being confined to the occasional moulding or dated inscription, as at Nos. 4–7 Dale Road (Rose Cottage), Coalbrookdale.

Stone buildings mostly date from the 17th century. They are few in number, which is surprising in view of the availability of good sandstone nearby. Better quality building, such as The Lodge, Ironbridge, have external walls built of coursed blocks of different height, and the stone is more finely worked than on lesser buildings, such as Nos. 58–59 Hodgebower, Ironbridge, where the walling is of uncoursed random rubble.

The lower part of the external walls of some early brick buildings is also built of stone. This occurs at The Tuckies House, Jackfield (Plate 61), where the east wing has a coursed sandstone base, and also in an early range of brick farm buildings at Hay Farm, Madeley. This form of construction may reflect the conservatism of local builders unused to building in brick, and uncertain of its structural stability.

Brick superseded both timber and stone as the usual building material after *c.* 1700.[89] It soon became established and used for houses of all grades. Brick was manufactured locally from the abundant supplies of clay that were exposed along the banks of the River Severn. The main centre of production was around Broseley and Jackfield.[90]

Brickwork of the early 18th century is irregular, the size of bricks varies, and they are often uneven in texture and shape. In order to overcome surface variations, mortar joints tend to be thick. These older bricks are generally of a red-brown colour; typical dimensions are 230mm. (9in.) by 57mm. (2¼in.) by 102mm. (4in.), five courses rising 343mm. (13½in.), as at No. 11 Jockey Bank, Ironbridge, (*c.* 1720).

The introduction of the brick tax in 1784 led eventually to the manufacture of larger bricks.[91] These are often over 76mm. (3in.) in height, as at No. 9 Darby Road, Coalbrookdale (*c.* 1790), where the dimensions are 235mm. (9¼in.) by 78mm. (3⅛in.) by 119mm. (4¼in.), five courses rising 435mm. (17¼in.). By this time bricks were becoming more even in shape and texture, with thinner joints between courses.

The best quality brickwork occurs on the more important 18th-century fronts, where window arches of rubbed brick are sometimes used. Flemish bond is used on nearly all buildings. The only exceptions are a few vernacular buildings where Flemish stretcher bond occurs, and also an isolated example of English garden wall bond.[92]

During the first half of the 19th century there was little variation in the size of bricks. The most common colour is a pale mottled brown. White bricks first appeared in the 1840s as dressings on two notable buildings in Ironbridge, Orchard House, and the Severn Wharf Building. At the same time vitrified brick headers were first used as a decorative feature on some house fronts, as at 13-14 Paradise, Coalbrookdale.

After 1860 machine-moulded bricks first appeared. They have a uniform shape and texture, and the common dimensions average 240mm. (9½in.) by 83mm. (3¼in.) by 122mm. (4¾in.), five courses rising 445mm. (17½in.). Blue bricks were also popular and were used for several of the larger buildings, including the Coalbrookdale Literary and Scientific Institution (1859),[93] Ironbridge National School (1859), and Ironbridge Police Station (1862).

Polychrome brick is less common, but was used for the Wesleyan Infant school, Madeley Wood (1858), and later for St. Mary's church, Jackfield (1863). Elsewhere it was used sparingly, for minor architectural embellishments, such as string-courses and dressings.

Plain Tile is the general roof covering. Some of the 17th-century vernacular houses have steep pitched roofs, which may have been thatched originally. Welsh slate is used prior to 1850 only for the largest buildings, but in the second half of the 19th century it is sometimes used for the more important detached houses.

Jackfield and Broseley excelled in the manufacture of roofing tiles. There are some good local roofs, including a most unusual design of Nos. 20-21 Buildwas

Road, Ironbridge (Plate 62), where the entire roof surface is enriched with polychrome pattern of zig-zags and diamond shapes. Geometrical tiling was used in bands on some of the better late-19th-century buildings, usually in conjunction with polychrome brick. Ornamental ridge crests also occur.

Cast-Iron was a radically new building material, first introduced for a range of architectural items in the fourth quarter of the 18th century. Very few of these cast-iron features are marked, but most are found in Coalbrookdale, and it seems logical to assume that they were made at the local ironworks. They include cast-iron window lintels and window sills, solid-frame cast-iron windows, cast-iron porches, and cast-iron chimney 'pots'. The use of cast-iron to manufacture what are, in effect, prefabricated factory-made building components was a very significant innovation. Its use was not confined to external items, but also included a number of interior fittings, including cast-iron kitchen ranges, cast-iron fireplaces, and cast-iron stair balusters.

Ground Stability

Builders in Ironbridge were faced with the formidable task of building against the steep hillside of the valley. Inevitably constructional problems arose. The underlying ground was unstable in places, and to create a flat building plot that was sufficiently large, it was often necessary to hack ground out of the hill slope, or else build the back of houses directly against the bank.[94] The latter practice created damp, unhealthy conditions and was deplored by enlightened opinion of the time.[95]

One method of securing land over small areas was the construction of flat terraces supported on arched brick vaults (a range of brick arches support a terrace of ground at the back of Nos. 15–16 Church Hill, Ironbridge). Despite all these efforts, attempts to secure a stable footing for external walls were often unsuccessful and several walls cracked and bulged where foundations failed. These failures have affected smaller vernacular buildings to a greater extent than the larger structures, such as schools, chapels and churches, which were sited with extreme care and built with very sound foundations.

Landslips were another hazard. Severe ground movement affected areas of the Gorge. A sheet-slide destroyed part of Jackfield in the winter of 1951–52, and a flow-slide occurred at Madeley Wood in 1935 destroying a whole section of the town.

Construction Details

In a few of the oldest brick buildings, dating from the early 18th century, the load of the main cross-beam supporting the first floor is carried by a timber lintel spanning the window opening.[96] Regulations were introduced in London in the 17th century to prevent beams being constructed on lintels or window heads in this manner.

It became common practice in the late 18th century to build long timbers into the gable brickwork of cottages with the intention of strengthening the structure. These bonding timbers can often be seen running below the level of the eaves in the outer gable wall. The technique has been proved to be unsatisfactory, as the wooden bonding timbers have tended to perish faster than the surrounding brickwork, leaving the upper gable unsafe.

A damp-proof course was built into the foundations of the Ironbridge National school (1859). It consists of a horizontal layer of impervious slate laid in the wall between the stone foundations and the upper wall of blue brick.

Chapter Seven

ARCHITECTURAL DETAILS

Dated Features

Three buildings have dated architectural features. A cartouche at Belmont House, Ironbridge (Plate 63), bears the initials J. and M.P., and is dated 1753, and a rainwater head at the Calcutts House, Jackfield, is inscribed with the initials J. and S.C. and dated 1755 (Plate 64). Finally, at the Hay Farm, Madeley, a circular cast-iron plaque in the north gable wall of the stable-block bears the date 1775 with the initials of Abraham Darby III.

Windows

Any assessment of window-glazing prior to 1700 is impossible, as no original mullion windows have survived in timber-framed buildings. It is probable that some windows were unglazed, with internal shutters only.

After 1700, with the advent of brick as the normal walling material, the proportion of window openings is vertical, and the mullion and transom window is the normal type (Plate 65 and Fig. 26). Most transoms are double-light windows, but a few triple-light transoms occur. Zinc bars are used for glazing in nearly all cases, and lead cames are rare. In the double-light transom it is usual for one of the lower lights to open. The wrought-iron casement frame is hung on hooks driven in to the window jambs and the window is locked by casement fasteners which engage the central mullion on the inside. Sometimes the inner edges of the mullion are given a simple decorative moulding.

Fig. 26   Double-light mullion and transom window

Transom windows generally have plain openings. It is normal to span the window head with a segmental arch laid of brick headers. Sills are rare. Occasionally window heads are given a more elaborate treatment. A Gothic design at Primrose Cottage, Coalbrookdale (Plate 42) and another at Nos. 20–21 Buildwas Road, Ironbridge, have pointed arches in conjunction with Y-shaped tracery. Better quality vernacular houses have segmental brick arches with projecting keystones; an arch of this type occurs in Jackfield dated 1750 (Plate 46).[97]

Most windows were originally fitted with shutters. These have generally been removed, but they still remain on a few houses. These are of the simplest kind, made of vertical boards held together at the back by horizontal ledges. Some shutters are framed, as at No. 1 Cherry Tree Hill, Coalbrookdale (Plate 71), a type more common on larger buildings.

Double-hung sash windows are introduced in the mid-18th century, first on the large fashionable fronts, and later among the smaller vernacular houses. Some buildings have had sash windows inserted in place of original mullion and transom

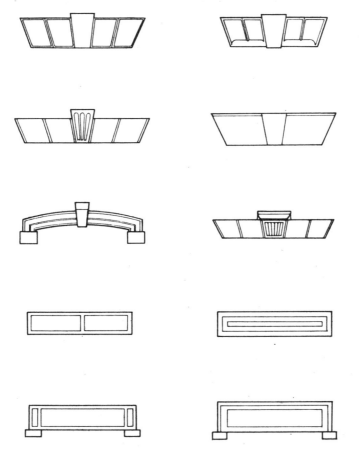

Fig. 27 Types of window lintel.

windows. On other buildings double-hung sashes are used for the principal elevation, but casements for subsidiary situations where they are not easily seen. The most elaborate sashes at the Market Building, Ironbridge (Plate 66), are tripartite Palladian windows set between slender pilasters and have narrow marginal sidelights. The east front of the *Tontine* hotel has similar windows and a matching Venetian window in the central bay. Early sash boxes are set well forward, almost flush with the external wall face, but by 1800 the standard practice is to recess them in a 115mm. (4½in.) reveal. Window openings in the better-quality fronts are generally spanned by flat arches of rubbed brick. Cheaper buildings have flat arches of common brick. It was not until the late 18th century that artificial stone lintels were introduced. The earliest design was the skew-back lintel with simulated voussoirs and a fluted central keyblock (Plate 67), but keyblocks generally are plain (Plate 68). In the 19th century a wide range of different lintel types was in use (Fig. 27).[98] A popular local design has a moulded segmental arch with central keyblock (Plate 69). Rectangular lintels (Plate 70) are also in extensive use.

A radical innovation in window construction took place in Coalbrookdale in the late 18th century, when the solid-frame cast-iron window was introduced.

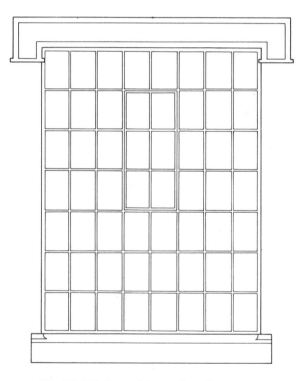

Fig. 28 Window with cast-iron frame, cast-iron sill, and cast-iron lintel, at the former mill, Coalbrookdale

It seems at first to have been regarded as an inferior type, and its use was confined to less important rooms. The company terraced rows, for example, have transom windows for house fronts, but cast-iron windows for the brewhouses. Later, cast-iron came into more widespread use and solid frame windows occur on some cottages, as at Nos. 1–2 Cherry Tree Hill, Coalbrookdale (Plate 71). Generally, however, it is for windows in industrial buildings, churches and chapels, that cast-iron was most popular.

Cast-iron is also used for window lintels and sills. The two finest examples are The Great Warehouse and the former Mill, Coalbrookdale (Plate 72 and Fig. 28), where cast-iron frames are used in conjunction with rectangular cast-iron lintels and sills. The most elaborate lintel design occurs at No. 31 Wellington Road, Coalbrookdale, which has recessed rectangular side panels and a projecting central keyblock (Plate 73).

The heads of cast-iron windows vary in shape. A few buildings have semicircular arched heads, as at The Old School, Coalbrookdale, and one example has an elliptical head, at The Wesleyan chapel, Coalford (1825). Smaller round-arched widows are frequently used for less conspicuous positions, at the back of cottages. The most common design has a fanlight head, and a four-pane, inset opening light (Plate 74 and Fig. 29).

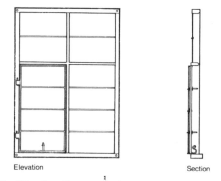

Elevation   Section

Fig. 29 Smaller type of cast-iron window

After 1830 window design is influenced by the Gothic Revival. The mullion and transom window comes back into favour, and casements reappear. These now have wooden glazing bars. Window openings have brick label moulds, and moulded brick sills are also in use (Plate 75). They first appear in the Parochial Infant school, Madeley Road, Ironbridge (1831), and later for larger residences such as Southside, Church Hill.

The Greek Revival style influenced the design of windows on a few house fronts after 1850. An instance is at No. 57 Belmont Road, Ironbridge (Plate 76), which has plain projecting architraves and a simple cornice carried on coarse console brackets. After 1860 windows with plain cornices and consoles begin to appear.

Crown glass window-panes continued to be made throughout the 18th and into the early 19th centuries. The surface is noticeably uneven with variations in thickness. Glazing bars on the best houses usually have a thin section, while

53

those on vernacular cottages are thicker. There are also variations in the size of panes. A typical pane size on an early cottage sash is about 200mm. (8in.) by 300mm. (12in.); this compares with a pane size of 305mm. (12in.) by 406mm. (16in.) used for the sashes of large 19th-century houses. it is not, however, until the second quarter of the 19th century that improvements in the manufacture of sheet and plate glass made the use of the much larger panes possible.

Doorways

The more important houses, built in the mid-18th century, have prominent door-cases. Architraves are moulded and usually have a rectangular or semi-circular window-light set between slender console brackets, with a pediment or shallow cornice above. Good examples of door-cases with pediments survive at The Grange, Darby Road, Coalbrookdale, and The Calcutts House, Jackfield; and there is a door-case with a shallow cornice at Belmont House, Ironbridge (1753). Other 18th-century door-cases are much plainer; those at No. 7 Darby Road, Coalbrookdale, and No. 11 The Wharfage, Ironbridge, have simple moulded architraves with ears, the latter recently restored.

The six-panel door was used for the best houses in the 18th century. The early panels were fielded, but in the 19th century they became flat with applied mouldings. By 1840 the four-panel door was in use and quickly gained in popularity. At the vernacular level doors were ledged and battened, but many have been replaced.

Door-cases with open pediments became popular in Coalbrookdale and Iron-bridge in the 19th century, and were used mostly for medium-size detached residences, where they formed part of a symmetrical front. The open pediment usually contains a radial fanlight, supported at the sides by slender pilasters which are plain. On a few door-cases, the fanlight is set between paterae placed at the top of each pilaster, as at the *Crown* inn, Hodgebower, Ironbridge, and Paradise House, Coalbrookdale (Plate 77). Reeding occurs at No. 26 Church Road, Coalbrookdale, but it is not common. Post-1830 door-cases are generally very plain (Plate 78) with a simple entablature. Sometimes, as at No. 11 Paradise, Coalbrookdale (Plate 79), the pilasters are panelled with a vertical moulding, but normally they are plain. It was usual in the 19th century to give the six panels of the traditional door a different treatment and often the upper four are fielded, or have raised mouldings, while the lower two are plain with a simple outer beading. The reveals are generally panelled in a similar way.

Some cottage doorways have a hood above the front entrance. This may be formed of a gabled pediment supported at the sides by carved console brackets. Another type is the flat canopy, which generally has more ornate mouldings. At The Lees, Coalport Road, Madeley (Plate 80), a thin cornice supported by finely-worked consoles had a fluted frieze (now destroyed). One of the best door hoods to survive is at No. 53 Wellington Road, Coalbrookdale (Plate 81), where the console brackets are richly carved in an elaborate moulding. Door hoods may have been added to some cottages in the late 18th and early 19th centuries.

Porches of delicately-worked cast-iron are rare. The best example, at Woodside House, Coalbrookdale (Plate 82), has an ornamental design in fretwork in the

Regency style. Only a few of the larger 19th-century houses have porches with freestanding columns. An example at No. 43 Darby Road has a plain entablature, with moulded cornice supported by Doric columns, all made of cast-iron.

One doorway of interest which falls outside the normal categories is a late 18th-century design at the *Tontine* hotel, Ironbridge (Plate 83), which has a shallow open pediment and radial fanlight above a double-leaf door and a pediment supported by two pairs of slender pilasters which contain narrow sidelights.

Eaves Cornices

Moulded eaves cornices are a feature of the large mid-18th-century residences. These are mostly of wood, but in one instance, at The Grange, Darby Road, of moulded ashlar. Moulded cornices with modillions are introduced first at Belmont House, Ironbridge in 1753. The subsidiary elevations of these houses have plain brick eaves.

Vernacular fronts are treated with greater simplicity. Until 1750 it is normal for the rafters to oversail the wall-plate at the eaves, a practice which gives a horizontal shadow line along the length of the projection. As the 18th century advanced it became more general to incorporate a brick oversailing course at the eaves. The most common type is of dentil brick, which consists of a course of alternately projecting headers (Plate 84). Less common is 'dog nosing', where the bricks are set diagonally and project at their end corners (Plate 85). A few of the better vernacular houses, such as No. 38 Church Hill, Ironbridge, have dentil eaves of moulded brick (Plate 86).

Chimneys

There are variations in the position of chimney-stacks in buildings erected before 1700. Some stacks are built against a gable wall, or placed laterally against the long wall, others have been inserted. Most of the stone stacks have been rebuilt in brick in the 18th century, and often chimney breasts project beyond the gable wall of these early vernacular buildings, as at Nos. 34–35 Belmont Road, Ironbridge. At Nos. 4–7 Dale Road (Rose Cottage), Coalbrookdale, a substantial brick stack was inserted in the centre of a timber-framed house in the early 18th century.

The finest 18th-century chimneys are a group of stacks at the Hay House, Madeley (Plate 87), which have blind round-headed arcading. Elsewhere, on the smaller vernacular buildings, the stacks are much plainer, and generally have simple caps with oversailing courses and tiled or arched-brick offsets. As the 18th century advanced there was an increasing tendency to place chimney stacks in the gable ends of double-fronted houses, where they sometimes projected. This position helped to give greater balance to the elevation and make it appear more symmetrical. Some stacks are unusually tall, particularly among the houses lining the lower slopes of the Gorge, the extra height giving the flues a greater draught and helping to carry smoke well clear of the valley (Plate 88).

Two of the best 19th-century chimneys occur on Gothic buildings erected in the 1840s. Both are of polychrome brick. Those at The Severn Wharf Building, Ironbridge (Plate 89), are in the form of castellated turrets and have terracotta pots, while those at The Orchard, Church Hill (Plate 90), have groups of clustered cylindrical stacks, some spirally grooved, and others with chevron patterning.

Cast-iron chimney 'pots' are widely used in Coalbrookdale, and probably date from the late 18th century (Plate 91). Almost certainly they were manufactured at the Coalbrookdale Company foundry, and they are cast to a similar design, each pot being square with the corners cut away.

String-Courses

Projecting brick string-courses are a feature of many house fronts in the first half of the 18th century. They appear on houses of all grades, from large detached residences, like Dale House, Darby Road, to smaller vernacular cottages, such as No. 11 Jockey Bank, Ironbridge. The string is usually three courses in depth, and there may be one at the level of the first floor and another above it at second-floor level. These brick string-courses are never carried around the corners of the building, but stop short at the ends of the elevation. In one instance, at No. 8 Darby Road, the central course of the string is composed of alternately projecting headers.

Gable Parapets

Gable parapets are a general roofing feature in the 18th century. Many have been taken down and roofed over in recent years. They are normally at least five courses in depth and incorporate an oversailing course. In a few instances the gable end is stepped.

Roof Structures

It is impossible to generalise about 17th-century roof structures on the limited evidence available. Two buildings in Ironbridge, at No. 3 Wesley Road, and No. 11 Jockey Bank, have gable trusses of similar design, with the collar carrying side purlins, and V-shaped struts supporting the upper ends of the principal rafters (Fig. 30).[99]

Many vernacular roofs do not contain service hatches, making any inspection of the structure impossible. Most appear to be collar roofs. Where the structure is visible, the timbers are generally of a thin scantling and the construction fairly crude. Purlins are sometimes made of unworked timbers, and occasionally these are visible, projecting at the gable end of a building. One late-18th-century house, Nos. 15–16 Church Hill, Ironbridge, is unusual in having a large central king-post truss, pegged to the tie-beam, with struts supporting the principal rafters (Fig. 30).

The construction of rear wings follows a standard roofing technique. The back roof is supported at the rear by valley boards which are fixed to the upper sides of the rafters (Plate 92). These boards help to give extra support at the junction with the main roof.

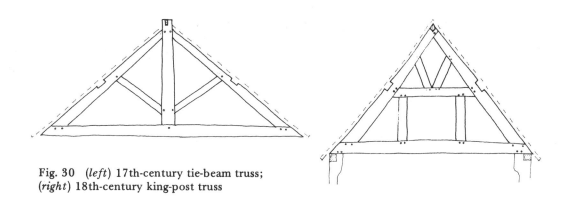

Fig. 30 (*left*) 17th-century tie-beam truss;
(*right*) 18th-century king-post truss

Staircases

Staircases form important architectural features in the larger buildings. The oldest, at the Tuckies House, Jackfield (Plate 93), is of late 17th-century type. It has heavy turned bulbous balusters, closed strings, and square newel posts (which rise above the level of the handrail). A fine mid-18th-century staircase at the Calcutts House, Jackfield (Plate 94) has a moulded handrail, two balusters to each tread, square knops and open strings. The balustrade has newel posts. Balusters of cast-iron with very slender shafts are used at the *Tontine* hotel, Ironbridge (Plate 95), in the late 18th century. These are square on plan, and simply moulded, with two to each tread. Newels are omitted and the handrail is curved at the corners. One staircase of interest, dating from the third quarter of the 19th century, is at the offices of the Coalbrookdale Company (Plate 96). It consists of slender cast-iron balusters with a handrail which is swept round at the bottom to a decorative cast-iron newel, surmounted by a female figure supporting a lamp-holder in the form of a torch.

Fireplaces

Fireplaces have most often been removed and replaced, so that few 18th-century examples remain. Two matching fireplaces in the assembly rooms of the *Tontine* hotel, Ironbridge (Plate 97), are probably the work of local craftsmen working from a copy book. The composition is classical, with fluted pilasters, volutes to the capitals and a central frieze tablet, but the carving is crudely executed and has a vernacular quality.

Fireplaces with pinewood architraves are enriched with applied composition decoration during the late 18th century. A good example in Ironbridge (Plate 98), has an elaborate frieze composed of wheatsheaf ornament, divided by bands of fluting, and honeysuckle decoration applied to each pilaster. Very occasionally cottage mantlepieces are carved (Plate 99), but this is exceptional.

Cast-iron fireplace surrounds were first introduced in the 19th century. They are rarely marked, but were almost certainly produced at the Coalbrookdale works. The most elaborate design, at the Calcutts House, Jackfield, is classical

57

in style, having attached Ionic columns, a frieze with anthemion decoration, and a central tablet with decorative garlands. A simpler design has a frieze with an intricate floral design enriched with leaf ornament.

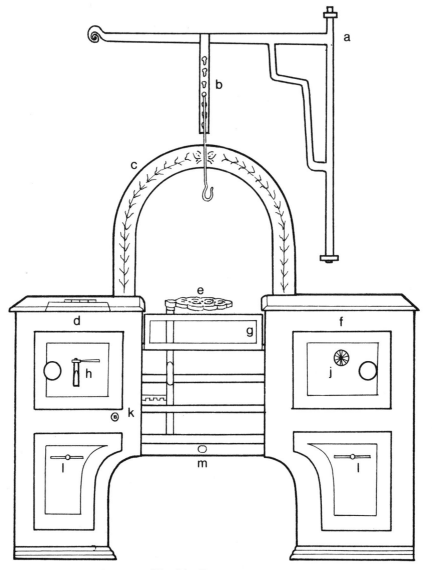

Fig. 31 Cottage range

Key

a = Crane
b = Pot hook
c = Semi-circular cast-iron back-plate
d = Boiler
e = Trivet
f = Oven

Key

g = Fall bar
h = Brass cock-tap
j = Brass ventilator
k = Winding cheek
l = Damper
m = Draw-out slide

Occasionally cottages still have cast-iron kitchen ranges, some bearing the mark of the Coalbrookdale Company. The cottage range (Plate 102 and Fig. 31) is the most common type and occurs in seven different sizes, each with a sham of different width. The hobs on these ranges are generally canted, and the grate has an arched cast-iron head. The better ranges normally have stirrup drop handles (Plate 103), and are more elaborate. In the finest castings the entire front, and sometimes the back plate of the cover, is enriched with decoration (Plate 104). This may take the form of a classical moulding, the quality of some of the work being remarkably high. One oven door (Plate 105), for example, has anthemion decoration at the angles, and another (Plate 106), has decoration in the form of lion masks on the door and sham.

Other Architectural Details

Interiors have frequently been altered and in some cases only the shell of the original building survives.

Floors in most vernacular houses are covered with tile quarries in the living-room. These vary in size, but the normal flooring tile is between 152mm. (6in.) and 228mm. (9in.) square, and laid directly on to a smooth earth surface. Parlours occasionally have elm boarding, or a superior finish of brick paviours laid in a herringbone pattern.

Arched recesses are often built into solid earth at the back of houses to stabilise the ground. These may form a store, pantry or rear service-room, and are commonly composed of segmental-arched, brick vaults.

Cellars occur in some 17th-century houses, and appear in some numbers in the 18th and 19th centuries.[100] The older cellars generally have external access.

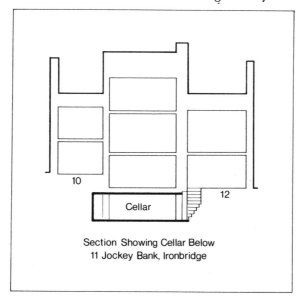

Fig. 32   Cellar, No. 11 Jockey Bank, Ironbridge

59

That at No. 11 Jockey Bank, for example, is approached via the living room of No. 12 (Plate 107 and Fig. 32). There is no evidence that these cellars were used as dwellings:[101] they may simply have formed storage space. Cellar roofs are generally constructed of brick vaulting.

Wells form internal features in many small houses. They are often located in a service-room at the back of the house, and consist of a small square opening giving access to a water-chamber with lined side walls. There are variations in the depth of these chambers, but 1.5m. (5ft.) is normal.

Locks and **Hinges** are often of some interest. A simple late 18th-century cottage lock is illustrated in Plate 108 and Fig. 33. The wrought-iron spring acts upon a

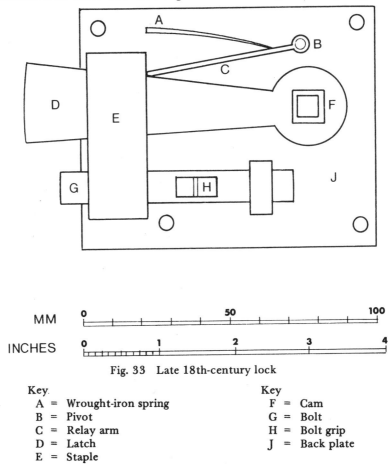

Fig. 33   Late 18th-century lock

Key		Key	
A =	Wrought-iron spring	F =	Cam
B =	Pivot	G =	Bolt
C =	Relay arm	H =	Bolt grip
D =	Latch	J =	Back plate
E =	Staple		

brass relay arm which depresses the latch. The cam of the latch has a squared section to fit the knob shaft which passes through it. Wrought-iron 'H' and 'L' hinges were general in the 18th century for interior doors, but cast-iron butt hinges supplanted them in the 19th century.[102]

Encaustic Tiles are used as a wall and floor covering in some buildings. They are of 19th-century date, and are almost certain to be the product of one of two former manufacturers: either Maw and Co., or Craven Dunnill, Ltd., of Jackfield. There is a good example of an encaustic tile wall-covering at the former Severn House (the *Valley* hotel), Ironbridge, which in the late 19th century was the home of Arthur Maw of Maw and Co., Ltd.[103]

Door Furniture is generally of 19th-century origin. Many of the designs must have been catalogue items as they can be seen in other parts of England. One of the earliest patterns is a cast-iron letterbox, having a broad ornamental border and fleurs-de-lis motifs at the angles (Plate 109). The more refined knockers are classical and decorated with festoons (Plate 110). Cottage doors frequently have Norfolk latches. These have full-length mounting plates and occasionally handles with a full-round grasp-band forming a decorative collar (Plate 111).[104] In the 19th century latches are generally of cast-iron, but the earlier 18th-century examples are hand-forged.

Rainwater Goods have mostly been added to vernacular buildings in the 19th century. They are of cast-iron and in some instances supported by wrought-iron brackets (Plate 112). Some of the larger 18th-century houses have wooden gutters which are lined with lead.

Chapter Eight

GENERAL

Street Furniture

Several items of cast-iron street furniture have survived. These include a **water conduit** (Plate 113) at Church Hill, Ironbridge, which has a fluted shaft, and decoration in the form of a lion mask, domed cover and finial; a **mile plate** (Plate 114), set in a wall adjoining the Wharfage at Ironbridge; two **boundary plates** (Plate 115) which mark the limits of the Hay Farm in Coalport; a circular cast-iron **bench-mark** attached to a gate pier at the entrance to the Coalbrookdale Ironworks; and a small **plate** fixed to the gable wall of No. 1 Dale End, Coalbrookdale, which is inscribed 'Feb. 12 1795 A Flood on the Severn came to the top of this plate'.

Gas was first introduced to Ironbridge in 1839. The works were situated near to the Madeley Wood Company's brick-works on Waterloo Road, and the streets of Ironbridge were first lit with gas on 5 November 1839.[105] Very few of the original street fittings have survived, although there are still several gas mantles to be seen inside houses. A pair of original **lamp-posts** survive in Coalbrookdale, one at the entrance to the Coalbrookdale Company works, and the other further down the valley at Dale End. Both were erected in 1897 to commemorate the Diamond Jubilee of Queen Victoria. They are similar in style, having Corinthian-type capitals, but the original gas lanterns have been removed.

Formerly a public **drinking fountain**, erected in 1863, stood in the Market Square at Ironbridge. It took the form of a 15ft.-high granite obelisk, and stood on a stone base. Water was piped nearly a mile to feed two taps and a dog trough.[106]

Apart from these items, several sets of cast-iron and wrought-iron **gates and railings** were erected. Many of these are still standing, including two elegantly-designed entrance gates to alleyways at the side of shops in the High Street and Tontine Hill, Ironbridge (Plate 116). A notable range of boundary gates run along the perimeter of the Coalbrookdale Literary and Scientific Institution which are contemporary with the main building (1859). The gate piers are styled with heavy mid-Victorian detailing, and have attached shafts, round-headed tops and spearhead finials. More delicate sets of gates and railings are to be seen along some of the better domestic frontages, as at South View, Church Hill, Ironbridge (Plate 117).

Sanitation

In most houses this traditionally took the form of an outside earth closet. Some of these still survive, and a few are supplied with twin-hole seats. A closet of this type, at the Hay House, is located in the attic with a garderobe shoot beneath. In the 19th century there were innovations. The correspondent of the *Shrewsbury Chronicle* noted at the opening of the Wesleyan Infant school at Madely Wood in 1859 that the 'lavatory, for the use of the children . . . is plentifully supplied with soft water by means of a pump, and fitted up with a slate slab and iron enamelled basins with plugs and washers'.[107] Provision generally fell well short of this, and Randall noted in 1880 the 'sad deficiency of water' and complained of the amount of sewage thrown in the river.[108]

Gardens

The remains of two large landscaped gardens survive. A mid-18th-century engraving[109] shows a pleasure boat floating on the Upper Furnace Pool. This pool appears to have formed part of an extensive ornamental park which stretched along Loamhole Dingle, below Darby Road. A 19th-century print[110] shows that a prominent feature of this garden was a miniature cast-iron replica of the Iron Bridge, which linked Green Bank Farm with Darby Road across the waters of the Upper Furnace Pool. The other large ornamental garden was laid out on Lincoln Hill by William Reynolds for the use of workers.[111] This intricate maze of pathways and steps, originally known as the 'Workman's Walks', still climbs through the woodland on the steep hillsides above the River Severn.

The Setting

The construction of the Iron Bridge in 1779 was a remarkable technological achievement, and the town that quickly grew up above it was equally spectacular. It was a surprising site on which to build. The topmost land formed an undulating plateau, but most of the houses were built on the hillside, which fell sharply and unevenly from the summit. It was on these steep precipitous slopes that new buildings rose up in the late 18th and 19th centuries.

The odd shape of the terrain has left its mark. Nothing is regular. Roads cut across one another as they zig-zag uphill. The profiles of buildings are seen from unusual angles, in outline from above, or in silhouette from below. Cottages stand perched on ridges or clinging to the steeply-rising ground. In this setting the grouping of buildings is particularly striking, and the street pattern constantly changes from one viewpoint to the next.

Now that many of the buildings are empty, the Gorge has a strangely hard-bitten quality. Decay has reduced parts of the district to semi-dereliction, and vegetation grows among the crumbling walls. This dilapidation is offset by the renovation of some older buildings, but still whole sections of the Gorge are falling into ruin. This ghost-like setting makes the Gorge a set piece of the industrial picturesque.

Town and country are never clearly separated. Buildings are slotted next to gardens and fields, so that there are few continuous street frontages. The pattern is broken, and each building forms part of a much wider landscape which man has completely transformed over the last 200 years.

It is in this landscape, battered by centuries of industrial exploitation and subsequent neglect, that we can now glimpse with unique insight the fabric of an industrial community which has all-but vanished. Fortunately, by a fluke survival, we are left with a stunningly rich array of older buildings. But beyond their immediate architectural appeal lies their lasting importance as tangible physical evidence of the living conditions and aspirations which accompanied the formative stages of the industrial revolution in England.

REFERENCES

1.   J. D. Porteous, 'Urban Genesis and Development: the Case of Canal Created Ports' (Univ. of Hull Ph.D. thesis, 1969). These include Runcorn (1771-76), Stourport (1771), Ellesmere Port (1795), and Goole (1826),

2.   J. Plymley, *A General View of the Agriculture of Shropshire* (1803), 315.

3.   B. Trinder, *The Industrial Revolution in Shropshire* (1973), 222.

4.   Minute Book of the Proprietors of the *Tontine* hotel. Shrewsbury Borough Library. MS. 245/6.

5.   C. Hulbert, *The History and Description of the County of Salop* (1837), 343-48.

6.   E. T. Svedenstierna, *Svedenstierna's Tour of Great Britain 1802-3* (1973, English reprint), 65. Also W. A. Smith, 'A Swedish View of the West Midlands in 1802-1803', *West Midland Studies*. 3 (1969), 46. 'On the same side, below the iron bridge, houses extend for some considerable distance, in fact as far as Coalbrookdale . . .'

7.   T. Slaughter, 'Plan of Coalbrookdale; A Table of Buildings', 1753. MS. Coalbrookdale Museum Collection. Reproduced in A. Raistrick, *Dynasty of Ironfounders* (1953), facing 74.

8.   Kelly & Co., *Post Office Directory of Shropshire* (1856), 75. Nos. 1, 2 and 3, and No. 37 Coalport Road are said to be survivors of a range of brick buildings which formerly enclosed a central quadrangle. Ministry of Housing and Local Government List. No. HB91650/290/274/2, 15.

9.   *The Victoria County History of Shropshire* (1908), Vol. I, 442-46.

10.   J. Randall, *The History of Madeley* (1880), 351.

11.   J. Morduant Crook, 'The Pre-Victorian Architect: Professionalism and Patronage', *Architectural History*. 12 (1969), 62-80.

12.   M. H. Port, *Six Hundred Churches: The Church Building Commission 1818-1856* (1961). Also B. F. L. Clarke, *Church Builders of the Nineteenth Century* (1938), 20-21.

13.   J. W. Wragg, *St. Luke's Church, Ironbridge* (1937), 7.

14.   J. W. Wragg, *op. cit.*, 6-7. Thomas Smith also designed two other Commissioners' Churches: Christ Church, Wellington, Salop. (1838), and Christ Church, Brierley Hill, Staffs. (1845-6).

15.   J. W. Wragg, *op. cit.*, 6.

16.   *Illustrated London News*, 24 January 1852, 67. *Watton's Newspaper Cuttings*, Vol. 12, 135. Shrewsbury Borough Library and also M. H. Port, *op. cit.*, 158-9 give Reeves and Butcher as architects.

17.   *Shrewsbury Journal*, Wednesday, 26 Aug. 1863, 6. The old church of St. Mary, Jackfield (now demolished) was abandoned in the 19th century as ground movement factured the outer walls. The building was deconsecrated, but not demolished. It was standing in 1960 when it was photographed by the National Monuments Record (Ref. AA60/3013).

18.   B. F. L. Clarke, 'Street's Yorkshire Churches and Contemporary Criticism', *Concerning Architecture: Essays on Architectural Writers and Writing* (1968), 214 and 223. (St. John the Evangelist, Howsham.)

19.   J. Randall, *The History of Madeley* (1880), 132. B. Trinder, *The Industrial Revolution in Shropshire* (1973), 269-70.

20.   B. Trinder, 'The Methodist New Connexion in Dawley and Madeley', *Wesley Historical Society (West Midlands Branch) Occasional Publications* (1967), No. 1, 16–17 and 19.

21.   Madeley Wood Chapel Trustees Minutes, 6 March 1837. Shropshire County Record Office.

22.   A photograph of this old chapel can be seen in the Coalbrookdale Archives Collection (CBDA 394), Ironbridge Gorge Museum Trust.

23.   E. Cassey & Co., *Gazetteer and Directory of Shropshire* (1874), 569.

24.   Minute Book of Guardians of Madeley Union Workhouse, Vol. 6 (1861–72), 134–6; Shropshire County Record Office.

25.   J. Randall, *The History of Madeley* (1880), 246.

26.   J. Randall, *op. cit.*, 247.

27.   *Shrewsbury Journal*, Wednesday, 19 November 1862, 6.

28.   J. Randall, *The History of Madeley* (1880), 351.

29.   The Local History section of Shrewsbury Borough Library contains a good collection of late 19th-century plate photographs of Ironbridge.

30.   The Madeley Tithe Apportionment Map, dated 29 September 1849, in the Shropshire County Record Office, marks this warehouse.

31.   A beam on the ground floor is marked '1838'. The warehouse must surely have been built long before then. Perhaps the interior was remodelled and a new clock-tower added, somewhere between 1838–43.

32.   The Coalbrookdale Archives (CBDA 143a), Ironbridge Gorge Museum Trust, contain a photograph of the original design, with pediment.

33.   See the very pertinent remarks of Prof. A. Everitt, at the Historical Geography Research Group Meeting: Rural/Urban Interrelationship (Oxford 1972), reported in *Urban History Newsletter*, ed. H. J. Dyos (Autumn 1972), Nos. 18, 20.

34.   'Tontine' means 'loan or fund the surviving subscribers of which receive annuities increasing as they become fewer' (*O.E.D.*).

35.   Minute Book of the Trustees of the Iron Bridge 1775–98, 9 December 1785. Shrewsbury Borough Library, MS. 3689.

36.   Minute Book of the Proprietors of *Tontine* hotel, 18 July 1788. Shrewsbury Borough Library, MS. 245/6. A biographical note on Haycock appears in H. N. Colvin, *A Biographical Dictionary of English Architects* 1660–1840 (1954), 476–7.

37.   It was decided at a meeting of the proprietors of the *Tontine* hotel to extend the building (3 March 1786). The subsequent entries are ambiguous, but it appears that Samuel Wright acted as both surveyor and architect for the extension. Wright also submitted an estimate in 1783 for a new schoolroom at Bridgenorth Grammar School. *The Victoria County History of Shropshire* (1973), Vol. 2, 142n.

38.   E. Cassey & Co., *Gazetteer and Directory of Shropshire* (1874), 557–8.

39.   B. Trinder, *The Industrial Revolution in Shropshire* (1973), 332.

40.   See M. Anderson, 'Education and the Factory in Industrial Lancashire 1780–1840'. *Economic History Review* (1967), 266–79.

41. M. Seaborne, *The English School its Architecture and Organisation 1370–1870* (1971), 211.

42.   J. Randall, *The History of Madeley* (1880), 300n.

43.   M. Seaborne, *op. cit.*, 198.

44.   M. Seaborne, *op. cit.*, 200–211;

45.   School Plans, submitted to the Department of Education and Science for Building Grants. Shropshire County Record Office. MS. 1564/1–432.

46.   *Shrewsbury Chronicle*. Friday, 7 January 1859, 7. James Wilson, known as 'Wilson of Bath', designed various churches in North Somerset between 1843 and 1861. In Bath he was responsible for the Church of Christ Scientist, Charlotte Street (1845); Kingswood School (1851); the Royal School (1856–8); and the Church of St. Paul, Monmouth Street (1873).

47.   This is clear from the School Plans. See note 45.

48.   E. Kelly & Co., *Post Office Directory of Shropshire* (1879), 335.

49.   *Shrewsbury Chronicle*, Friday, 3 June 1859.

50.   B. Trinder, *The Darbys of Coalbrookdale* (1974), 40.

51.   J. E. C. Peters, *The Development of Farm Buildings in Western Lowland Staffordshire up to 1880* (1969), 260. A similar design is recorded at Barnfields, Baswich.

52.   A common practice in the 19th century. See N. Harvey, *A History of Farm Buildings in England and Wales* (1970).

53.   Instances among the larger houses occur at The Lodge, Ironbridge. The Tuckies, Jackfield; Belmont House, Ironbridge; and Dale House, Coalbrookdale.

54.   R. W. Brunskill, *Illustrated Handbook of Vernacular Architecture* (1970), 25-26.

55.   H. E. Forrest, *The Old Houses of Wenlock* (1914), photograph facing p. 17.

56.   Plan of Part of Coalbrookdale, by G. Young of Worcester, 1786. Shropshire County Record Office. Cooper (Broseley) Calendar. Ref. p. 195, MS. 1681. Marks 'Pan Shops' at Dale End.

57.   House deeds show that the property remained a parcel of land with orchard, garden house, and mushroom house, until 26 December 1842, when the land was purchased by the Jackfield brickmaker, William Davis. The house he built is depicted in an engraving by William Spreat of Exeter, probably executed between 1842-49. The house was certainly completed by 1849, when it appears on the Tithe Apportionment Map. Later in the 19th century the house was occupied by the industrialist John Anstice, and later still, Henry Powell Dunnill of Craven Dunnill, Ltd.

58.   *Shropshire Newsletter* (Shropshire Archaeological Society), No. 34. June 1968, 15.

59.   Sale Notice. 7 May 1907.

60.   For a much broader national picture see P. Eden, *Small Houses in England 1520-1820* (1969), and R. W. Brunskill, *Illustrated Handbook of Vernacular Architecture* (1970), 101-05.

61.   A common feature. J. Wood, *A Series of Plans for Cottages and Habitations of the Labourer* (1781), 7, recommends that a cottage should be close to a spring of water 'a circumstance to be much attended to; and if there be no spring, let there be a well'.

62.   P. Eden, *op. cit.*, 30-32. R. W. Brunskill, *op. cit.*, 104-5.

63.   Ministry of Housing and Local Government. Provisional List of Buildings of Architectural or Historic Interest. Ref. HB91650/290/274/2. September 1967.

64.   Minute Book of the Coalbrookdale Company 1789-97, 12 December 1793. Coalbrookdale Museum. MS. (CBD-59-82-3). 'The premises called Nailor's Row being held under lease for 997 years from 20 day of March 1733 are reported to want considerable repairs'.

65.   The inscription, copied by the occupier at the time of restoration, is reported as having read:

> Thomas Rose, Senr.
> Deborah Rose,
> Tho. Rose,
> Daniel Rose,
> A ? Rose,
> John Rose,
> Dec 6 1746

66.   S. Pollard, 'The Factory Village in the Industrial Revolution', *English Historical Review* (1964), Vol. 79, 516-19.

67.   C. W. Chalklin, *The Provincial Towns of Georgian England* (1974), 163-65.

68.   Minute Book of the Coalbrookdale Company 1789-97. *op. cit.*, 19 November 1790. 'Agreed that all Dwelling Houses and Warehouses belonging to this Concern shall be measured and Valued and a rent fix'd upon them at the Rate of 7½ p. cent. on the Value.'

69.   Ruskin seems to have been among the first to advocate this. See E. Moberley Bell, *Octavia Hill* (1924), 76.

70.   Minute Book of the Coalbrookdale Company 1789-97. *op. cit.*, 26 September 1794.

71.   Minute Book of the Coalbrookdale Company 1789-97. *op. cit.*, 8 May 1794. Rent given as '28/- p. month'.

72.   Minute Book of the Coalbrookdale Company 1789-97. *op. cit.*, 26 September 1794.

73.   J. Farington, 'Coalbrookdale with Upper Forge and Pool, New Furnace, Lower Furnace Pool, Old Furnace and Jigger Bank, 1789'. Pencil sketch. Coalbrookdale Museum.

74.   Map of Coalbrookdale referring to the annexed lease from Mr. Reynolds to Coalbrookdale Company, 25 June 1794. Shrewsbury Borough Library. MS. 1618. Box 138. First noted by J. M. Wood, 'Company Housing for the Shropshire Ironfounders' (Liverpool Polytechnic RIBA dissertation 1974.)

75.   Segmental arches of this type have also been noted in Wales. J. B. Lowe and D. N. Anderson, *Iron Industry Housing Papers*, No. 1. Stack Square and Engine Row, Blaenavon, Monmouthshire (1972), 6.

76.   *Shropshire Newsletter* (Shropshire Archaeological Society), No. 33, 8. Mr. H. King and the Birmingham University Social History of Coalbrookdale Group very kindly gave me access to this material.

77.   Corner fireplaces are also noted in Wales. J. B. Lowe and D. N. Anderson, *Iron Industry Housing Papers*, No. 6. Bunker's Row, Blaenavon, Monmouthshire (1973), 49. They are not an innovation in domestic design: see, for example, W. A. Pantin, 'The Development of Domestic Architecture in Oxford', *Antiquaries Journal*, Vol. XXVLL. (1947), 132.

78.   B. Trinder, 'Coalbrookdale' (2.02), a guide published by the Ironbridge Gorge Museum Trust (1973), 6.

79.   B. Trinder, *The Darbys of Coalbrookdale* (1974), 68.

80.   The sequence in which these five terraces were built is not known. Differences in layout and design probably indicate that Charity Row was the first terrace to be erected. Possibly it was built as a company almshouse by the ironworks and, proving successful, adopted as the general housing type, to solve the pressing problem of having to accommodate large numbers of new workers. Certainly there was nothing new in the *idea* of terraced housing. Rows of this type had been built as almshouses throughout the 17th century in other parts of England; as, for instance, at Farncombe, Surrey, where one long brick terrace of ten dwellings had been built in 1622 by Richard Wyatt.

81.   Census Returns of 1851: Parish of Madeley. Shrewsbury Borough Library.

82.   See, for instance, Bunker's Row, Blaenavon, *op. cit.*, 6, where the floor area was 19.5 sq. m.

83.   From data available in the mid-19th century this does not seem to have been the case (though by that date the position may have changed). See. M. W. Hunt, 'Squatter Settlements in the Coalbrookdale Area' (Liverpool Polytechnic RIBA dissertation 1974).

84.   Single-storey 'barrack houses' characteristic of the northern part of the coalfield, in Donnington and Lilleshall, in the second half of the 18th century do not seem to have been built in Coalbrookdale. A single example survives at Cherry Tree Hill. See B. Trinder, *The Industrial Revolution in Shropshire* (1973), 323.

85.   It would also be interesting to know more about the role of the ironmaster Richard Reynolds in the provision of housing. See J. Plymley, *A General View of the Agriculture of Shropshire* (1803), 344. 'He has built many comfortable houses for old and distressed persons, and granted a great number of leases of waste land, in the proportion, if I recollect right, of about one-eighth of an acre to each person, to build on, they paying a fine of five guineas for a lease of ninety-nine years, and five shillings a year ground rent.'

86.   H. W. Forrest, *The Old Houses of Wenlock* (1922), 100 and plate facing 97.

87.   N. W. Alcock, *A Catalogue of Cruck Buildings* (1973), 50. First noted in *Shropshire Newsletter* (Shropshire Archaeological Society), No. 38, June 1970, 20, by M. Moran.

88.   For a national comparison, see J. T. Smith, 'Timber Framed Buildings in England', *Archaeological Journal* (May 1966), Vol. 122.

89.   This is an approximate date due to the lack of any clearly dated examples. Compare it with the date of 1660 put forward for the East Midlands by M. W. Barley, 'Farmhouses and Cottages', *Economic History Review* (1954-5), Vol. 7, 294.

90.   J. Randall, *The Clay Industries . . . on the Banks of the Severn* (1877). Reprinted 1974 by Salop County Library.

91.   See K. Hudson, *Building Materials* (1972), 29-30, for a general note on this tax. During the construction of the *Tontine* hotel in 1784 an allowance was paid to the builder,

Mr. Roden, for additional expenses incurred due to the tax. (Minute Book of the Proprietors of the *Tontine* hotel, 23 July 1784. Shrewsbury Borough Library. MS. 245/6.) There was a remission in the case of ecclesiastical buildings, and the estimated saving in the construction of St. Luke's church, Ironbridge, was £250. (J. W. Wragg, *St. Luke's Church, Ironbridge* [1937], 8.)

92. Carpenters' Row, Coalbrookdale.

93. These 'blue' bricks were made at the Coalbrookdale Company's own brickworks.

94. The so-called 'Back-to-Earth' house.

95. J. Wood, *A Series of Plans for Cottages or Habitations of the Labourer* (1781), 4.

96. As at No. 17 Church Hill, Ironbridge, and No. 11 Jockey Bank, Madeley Wood.

97. At No. 183 High Street, Jackfield.

98. Compare this with the range to be seen in York. See section by E. Gee, *Royal Commission on Historical Monuments (England). York* (1972), Vol. 3, xcix.

99. Tie-Beam trusses of this type without the V-shaped struts are a feature of 17th-century timber-framed buildings in Worcestershire. See F. W. B. Charles, 'Timber-Framed Buildings', in N. Pevsner, *The Buildings of England: Worcestershire* (1968), 63.

100. The Borough of Wenlock (Madeley Sanitary Division) Clearance Orders (Shropshire County Record Office), show a number of houses in which the cellars overlap. For instance, the cellar of No. 6 Jockey Bank was built under the living-room of No. 5 (Clearance Order No. 7); the larder of No. 54 Wesley Road was beneath No. 55 (Clearance Order No. 8); and the cellar of No. 4 The Lloyds was built under No. 6 (Clearance Order No. 13).

101. As for example in Liverpool in the 19th century. See J. H. Treble, 'Liverpool Working Class Housing (1801-1851)' in S. D. Chapman (ed.), *A History of Working Class Housing— A Symposium* (1971), 186-99.

102. Very little has been written on this subject. The best source book is J. Moxon, *Mechanick Exercises* (1703), section on smithing 18-31. In Canada, The Association for Preservation Technology has printed relevant articles in its quarterly journal, e.g., D. Streeter, 'Early American Wrought Iron Hardware, English Iron Rim Locks: Late 18th and Early 19th Century Forms', *A.P.T.* (1974), Vol. VI, No. 1, 41-65.

103. J. Barnard, *Victorian Ceramic Tiles* (1972) gives information on Maw & Co., 15, 33, 37, and Craven Dunnill, Ltd., 159.

104. For Norfolk and Suffolk Latches generally, see D. Streeter, 'Early American Wrought Iron Hardware', *A.P.T.* (1971), Vol. III, No. 4, 12-30.

105. E. Cassey & Co., *Gazetteer and Directory of Shropshire* (1874), 569.

106. *Shrewsbury Journal.* 29 April 1863.

107. *Shrewsbury Chronicle*, 7 January 1859, 7. (The Committee of Council on Education had stressed in 1848 the importance of proper sanitation in schools.)

108. J. Randall, *The History of Madeley* (1880).

109. F. Vivares and G. Perry, 'A View of Upper Works at Coalbrookdale 1758', engraving. Ironbridge Gorge Museum Trust. Reproduced as Plate 2 in B. Trinder, *The Industrial Revolution in Shropshire* (1973), facing 69.

110. William Westwood, 'The Upper Part of Coalbrookdale'. Undated print by Graf and Soret. Colour print of original in Ironbridge Gorge Museum Trust Collection.

111. S. Smiles, *Industrial Biography* (1863), 95-6. 'At Madeley, near Coalbrookdale, where he brought a property, he laid out, for the express use of the workmen, extensive walks through the woods on Lincoln Hill, commanding beautiful views. They were called "The Workmen's Walks", and were a source of great enjoyment to them and their families, especially on Sunday afternoons.'